Continued from front flap

build-ups by which a flesh-and-blood
man is made into a public image. The
essence of the build-up is that it does
not prove. It assumes. Its ultimate
consequences can be disastrous or
funny or both. Here Mr. Galbraith
deals also with the role of nostalgia in
shaping our economic and social attitudes and in the third part he returns
more lightheartedly to the same
theme. He takes the reader first to
northern New England where New
Yorkers invest nostalgically in country inns whose service improves after
each bankruptcy, then on to his
native Canada to recall the impact of
royalty on some of the world's least
royal people.

Mr. Galbraith is the author of the
recent best-seller *The Affluent Society*,
and of two earlier books, *American
Capitalism* and *The Great Crash, 1929*.
In *The Liberal Hour*, he treats current
problems with seriousness, clarity,
and a delightfully ironic wit.

The

Liberal Hour

Also by

John Kenneth Galbraith

Modern Competition and Business Policy
American Capitalism: The Concept of Countervailing Power
A Theory of Price Control
Economics and the Art of Controversy
The Great Crash, 1929
The Affluent Society

The

Liberal Hour

John Kenneth Galbraith

HOUGHTON MIFFLIN COMPANY BOSTON
The Riverside Press Cambridge
1960

Portions of this book have previously appeared, usually in somewhat different form, in various magazines, as follows:

American Heritage: "The Care and Prevention of Disaster" (under the title "The Days of Boom and Bust"). © 1958 by American Heritage Publishing Co., Inc.

The Atlantic Monthly: "Was Ford a Fraud?" (under the title "The Mystery of Henry Ford"). Copyright © 1958, by The Atlantic Monthly Company.

The New York Times Magazine: "Farming an Abandoned Farm" and "The Build-up and the Public Man" (under the title "The Perils of the Big Build-up"). Copyright © 1953, 1954 by The New York Times Company.

The Reporter: "The Pleasures and Uses of Bankruptcy" and "The Wholesome Influence" (under the title "Royalty on the Farm"). Copyright © 1959 by John Kenneth Galbraith.

The Saturday Evening Post: "The Decline of the Machine" (under the title "Men and Capital"). © 1960 The Curtis Publishing Company.

The Riverside Press
CAMBRIDGE · MASSACHUSETTS
PRINTED IN THE U.S.A.

For the Blacks

ADLAI STEVENSON *once referred to the moment just before presidential elections when even the most obsolete men become reconciled, if briefly and expediently, to the machine age. He thought that this pause in normal conservative occupation might be called "the liberal hour."*

Acknowledgments

THIS VOLUME began as a series of lectures which I gave under the auspices of the Merrill Foundation for Advancement of Financial Knowledge at Grinnell College in Grinnell, Iowa in the spring of 1958.

Under the terms of the lectureship, the lectures were to be published but with generous allowance of time and opportunity for revision. I have used quite a bit of time and in the matter of revision I have gone from opportunity to license. This is partly because lectures, like sermons, do not make books. No matter how resonant and uplifting they sound, at least to the lecturer, during delivery, they remain unimpressive in print. Of the lectures I gave at Grinnell, three are here in reasonably recognizable form. The rest have been merged into others. I am in debt to my old and good friend Howard Bowen, the president of Grinnell, for providing me with the opportunity to assemble my ideas on the topics I discussed there and, as revised, in this book. Also, it was a most pleasant week.

A number of the other chapters have previously been published. Of these two appeared in *The Reporter*, two in *The New York Times Magazine*, one in *The Saturday Eve-*

ning Post, one in an earlier version in *American Heritage* and one, also in an earlier version, in *The Atlantic Monthly*. I am grateful to these journals for permission to reprint.

At all stages early and late I had the help of Catherine A. Galbraith. For her merciless intervention on matters of fact, taste and grammar I couldn't be more grateful.

The typing and retyping of the manuscript were in the deft hands of Lois Foster. All other matters, great and small, tedious and more tedious, which are involved in getting a book into print were managed with rare competence and even more exceptional charm by Andrea Williams.

J. K. G.

Cambridge, Massachusetts
April 1960

Contents

xi

Part Three

The Nostalgic Farmer

The

Liberal Hour

Introduction

The Liberal Hour

REASONABLE PERSONS may well differ over what is the major menace to our way of life in our time. There is Communism and also those who hold that it can be best extirpated by universal annihilation. The men who picture the American family poised in prayer around a Thanksgiving turkey with a word for life insurance, light beer or Coca-Cola worked gracefully into the text have a claim. So do the increasing numbers who defend low pecuniary interest on grounds of high moral principle — the industrial statesmen who selflessly resist wage increases to protect the community from inflation, and the large fruit and vegetable farmers who argue that minimum wages and working standards for migrant labor would be an interference with our treasured traditions of human liberty. Not for years, we should note, has anyone complained with candor that some reform would cost him money.

However, it is possible that our greatest danger, in these days of massive introspection, is from our terrible solemnity. For this is a serious source of inflexibility. Change and new evidence have a way of making previous convictions seem odd, even ridiculous. The reasonably relaxed man can accept correction without too grievous loss of dignity. But

the solemn man cannot. He may have heard that the truth
will set him free. But he rightly senses that it might also
make him seem silly.

I would hope that this book, or most of it, might be considered a contribution to a more relaxed debate. It deals
with matters about which no one can be entirely sure. Certainly no one in his senses would wish to be frozen for life
to a set of conclusions on how (say) to compete with Russia.
So while I have challenged some of the solemn myths by
which we are bound — and perhaps have not been everywhere kind to the solemn men who propound and perpetuate
them — I am willing, at least in principle, to be challenged
in turn.

2

Not that I suppose that all of the book merits debate.
Some of the subjects attracted my attention because they
seemed important, others because they seemed interesting.
In all they fall into three parts. The first section is concerned with questions which some will think of considerable
contemporary urgency — the terms of our competition with
the Soviet Union;[1] the transcendent importance of intellectual

[1] The chapter on this was, of course, written before the flight of the
U–2 and the collapse of the summit conference in May of 1960. When
I wrote it, I more or less automatically took the precaution of saying
that I was assuming peaceful, or anyhow nonmilitary, competition and
that I was not predicting it. On subsequent reflection, I am not sure
that this prudence was necessary. In this world, no other form of competition is consistent with civilized survival and it is unlikely that our
relations with the Soviets will soon be noncompetitive. And the lesson
of the U–2, or part of it, was that a narrow preoccupation with military
operations and objectives can do us grievous and enduring harm in the
larger and not less critical competition for nonmilitary esteem and
reputation.

capital and the obsolescence of our machinery for main-
taining it; the alienation of our economic society from art and
aesthetics and the considerable consequences of this; and
the old, old question of inflation. Some of these matters I
have touched on before [2] and then, on further reflection,
have found myself less impressed by what I had said than
by what I had failed to say. This is discouraging but it is a
familiar incentive to authorship.

The following part has to do with economic history. The
marriage of economics and history produces a hybrid which
regularly combines the inadequacies of both. For economists, history is a featherbed into which fall those who are
unfitted by temperament or training for economic theory,
econometrics, economic statistics or the other more rigorous
forms of economic scholarship. Historians invariably venture into economic questions with caution amounting to
diffidence — they must always, they believe, keep one eye
over their shoulder for an economist who is waiting to de-
stroy them. It takes a certain brashness to attack the accepted
economic legends but none at all to perpetuate them. So
they are perpetuated.

I am less concerned here with what we believe than with
the circumstances impelling us to dubious beliefs. However,
the errors of interpretation which I take up do seem to me
to be important and to have a continuing relevance in our
own time. After a hundred years, the South has not entirely
got over the habit of attributing its economic misfortunes to
the Civil War and the aftermath — an attribution for which
there is no supporting evidence. We did not learn during

[2] Notably in *The Affluent Society*. Boston: Houghton Mifflin, 1958.

the twenties how damaging the short business view in Washington can be, in the slightly longer run, to the businessman at home. The misapprehension of the nature of modern industrial society by most of the historians of the New Deal, especially in their treatment of NRA, continues to delay the development of a price stabilization policy that would be relevant to an economy of vast corporations and strong unions. We are much less interested in history than, for example, the British. But this does not necessarily mean that we are less influenced by it.

The last section is also concerned with matters — small enterprise and bankruptcy, the use and misuse of derelict land, the uses of royalty — which are commonly treated with considerable solemnity. However, these pieces are here mostly because they were agreeable to write. One of them, when published before, to my pleasant surprise brought more comment than anything of comparable length I have ever written. That was the treatise on farming an abandoned farm. For weeks after it appeared I was deluged with suggestions, criticisms and also invitations from similar farm operators (or nonoperators) from all over the eastern United States. I was left with the impression that the care and management of derelict land is a major avocation (often disguised as a vocation) of the American people. The United States Department of Agriculture should have a division devoted to it. Perhaps it might be created as a kind of memorial to Ezra Taft Benson, to whom all who love abandoned farms will be forever in debt.

Part One

Spacious Issues

I

The Strategy of Peaceful Competition

ONE OF THE new and comparatively encouraging phrases that have recently come into the language of international relations has been peaceful competition. We are being told, with that impressive combination of certainty and unction that we use when we do not know, that our relations with the Soviet Union will increasingly be governed by such competition. Since, in this world, we may safely seize on any encouraging trends without being unduly encouraged, we may hope that this will be so.

In any case, this is the only kind of competition on which anyone can reflect with any comfort. And we should not be without hope. Clearly there is a growing appreciation of the new dimensions of destruction by modern weapons. That these had changed the calculus of war was urged by the well qualified after Hiroshima and Nagasaki. Perhaps so large a lesson required time to sink in. And certainly we were fortunate in having had these years during which it could penetrate the refractory materials protecting the human intelligence. For one senses that even the professionally bellicose are becoming more restrained these days. Even the professorial global strategists — those whom World War II gave an exciting insight into the theory and attractively remote practice of mass destruction — have, one feels, been losing their enthusiasm for universal annihilation.

It would be wrong, surely, to imagine that this modest accretion of wisdom and caution is confined to our side of the Iron Curtain. Whatever the peculiarities of the Russian temperament or the Communist commitment to its faith, there is no reason to think that these include a predilection for high temperature incineration. This being so, perhaps we shall have an increase in peaceful caution and a diminution in bellicosity on both sides. But my purpose is not to argue for this prospect but to assume it and to examine the nature of the resulting behavior.

2

The goal of military competition is relatively simple, even though the common feature of military strategists from Darius to Hitler has been a grievous inability to make things go according to plan. The goal, if the occasion arises, is to subdue the enemy with a minimum of damage to yourself. Indeed war has become impractical because this simple goal has become impractical. With modern weapons, even given a considerable superiority, there is no way a country can minimize damage to itself — even its own weapons may, under some circumstances, do it irreparable harm. And planning is almost certainly now more subjective than ever, although the planner is protected by the unlikelihood that he will survive to learn that he was wrong.

The alternative to military competition, it is usually assumed, must be economic competition. The first having become too disagreeable, we turn to the next most unappetizing thing. As commonly envisaged, this competition amounts to a production contest. The Soviets seek to out-produce us so we must seek to outproduce them. They seek to surpass us so we must surpass ourselves. In this race, the prize is awarded to the country with the greatest annual increase in its Gross National Product.

In recent years our Gross National Product has been in-creasing at a rate of rather less than three per cent; the Soviet increase has been better than seven per cent. Those with a considerable sense of urgency say our immediate job is to raise our rate of growth and so to protect our con-siderable headstart. Those who wish to reassure us say not that we should allow the Soviets to overtake us but that their figures are wrong. A small but flourishing industry is now devoted to proving statistically that the Russians' growth isn't what it is cracked up to be. Its Mike Todd is Mr. Colin Clark, the Australian and Oxford economist, who all but establishes that Russia is going backward.

Our rate of economic growth has not been satisfactory in recent years. There has been unnecessary unemployment. Incomes of important groups have lagged. Our present ma-chinery of public finance gets revenues for urgent public purposes with ease only out of expanding revenues. Growth settles many other problems — of this let there be no doubt.

And the Soviets are, indeed, challenging us to a produc-tion race. They proclaim their intention of overtaking us in every park and factory. One of their most successful indus-tries must be the production of pictorial statistics for posting on walls. We certainly must assume they are serious.

But to imagine that our competition with the Soviets consists in meeting their production challenge would be a major mistake. Economic growth means one thing to the Soviets and something very different to us. To a point they can win by pursuing this goal; we shall surely lose if we do so.

The U.S.S.R. was until recent times a backward and mainly agricultural country with a low standard of living. In such a country, a rapid rate of industrial growth and a rapid increase in agricultural productivity are important. They allow for an increase in present living standards and pave the path for future advance. They enable increased investment in technical and scientific advance. They provide a surplus for overseas use in support of foreign policy. It would probably be foolish in this world to imagine that military calculations will be absent from the most peaceful of peaceful competition. To a point, increased industrial capacity has a bearing on military effectiveness. However, this is a relationship that is much misunderstood and I will return to it presently.

In the U.S.S.R. there is a special need for increased production in a world where other countries have a more advanced industrial plant and a much higher standard of living. For the demonstration effect, as economists have come to call it, of wealth and well-being in other countries creates a presumption of inferiority — of being second-best. Everywhere in the world this is the effect of American living standards. It operates with special force in a socialist or Communist country, for there inferiority in living standard carries the implication of inferiority of system.

But these considerations do not hold, and certainly not with equal force, for us. The Russians want more because we have more. But we must ask ourselves *why* we want more. There must be a better reason than merely seeking to keep ahead. A mere statistical race, in which we turn in the best results for the sake of the bars on the charts, would be a futile thing. It would stir us to no enduring sense of national purpose. It would arouse no enthusiasm save among the statisticians, and no one but a statistician would be able to judge between the competing claims of the statisticians as to who had won.

When we examine the industries we would be seeking to expand with greater economic growth, we see with even more force how little there is for us in such a contest. Would we seek to increase food production? Obviously not. Surpluses are already vast. Obesity is now rather more a problem than malnutrition, and far more ingenuity now goes into the packaging of food than the producing of it. (Even here the end is in sight. The unopenable package, the goal of the container industry, is just around the corner. Thereafter the package cannot be further improved.) Similarly the need for clothing is not pressing. We now design clothes for their aesthetic or exotic, but rarely for their protective, effect. An annual automobile output of eight or ten million cars is within sight. It will bring appalling problems of storage and driving space. More of our countryside will be subject to the ghastly surgery of the superhighway. And it is a question whether the discards, wrecks, and derelicts can be recycled fast enough to prevent a hideous metallic blot from spreading out from the service stations to cover the whole land.

Some will wish to suggest that there are many individuals

and families with insufficient food, poor clothing, bad hous-
ing, or who are subject to other kinds of privation. This is
true. And to provide decently for these people would require more production. But first of all these people require
the income or the education, health, skills and abilities
which enable them to earn the income with which to buy
that production. Given that income, the production that
satisfies it will be forthcoming. The income or the opportunity for access to income is the place we have to start.
There is no assurance merely from expanding output *per se*
that the benefit will accrue to those at the bottom of the
pyramid who need the goods the most.

3

It is commonly assumed that the Russians are investing in
industrial plant — steel capacity, machinery and machine
tools production, chemical plant — for the sake of expanding
their military power. The greater such investment, the
greater their power.

No one can know for sure what the Soviets have in mind.
And there is also the possibility that they, like us, are guided
in economic matters less by thought than by its inconvenience. What is reasonably certain is that they must be reaching the point where further increases in their industrial
capacity and output add but little to their military power.
In old-fashioned wars, in which steel was projected against
steel, there were limits to the amount of heavy industry that
could be brought into use against the enemy. In World
War II, Germany, with much less steel capacity than the
Soviets now have, had more than enough to equip her vast

armies. With slight effort, she could have produced more steel from her available capacity; much was used for low priority purposes.[1] But modern weapons, as they are graciously called, make far less use of steel or other heavy industrial capacity than the old-fashioned kind. Also steel provides no defense against them. Unless the Soviets expect, one day, to mobilize and equip the vast armies which operated in World War II from the Baltic to the Black Sea — and believe that the plants which would do so would be allowed to operate without hindrance — then further increases in their industrial capacity can have little military relevance. A much smaller industrial plant than ours did not keep the Soviets from forging far ahead of us in the development of rockets and missiles.

If the Russians are reaching the point of diminishing returns on the military value of industrialization, then we have almost certainly passed it. Apart from its effect on public revenues, purely quantitative growth in our industrial plant adds nothing that is essential to our military strength. A much better case can be made that it weakens military capacity. Such growth provides us with goods and gadgets which we quickly come to consider necessary and which we would surrender with vast reluctance in emergency. Some of them — the automobile is a warning — may be bringing the final atrophy of our physical capacities. We are reminded of how hard it was in Korea to learn to fight an enemy that didn't ride in jeeps. Other advances — oil furnaces, motor transport, highly specialized food production

---

[1] Burton H. Klein. *Germany's Economic Preparation for War.* Cambridge: Harvard University Press, 1959. See especially pp. 130 et seq.

— make us dependent to the death on intricate and highly vulnerable supply lines.

Finally it is said that production provides us with an exportable surplus which enables us to support our allies and to strengthen our position in the underdeveloped lands by contributing liberally to their development. But it is not a shortage of production that has been handicapping such efforts in the past. Rather it has been reluctance to employ production for these purposes — and to appropriate the necessary funds. And as this is being written, another problem is on the horizon. That is the high cost of much of our industrial output — a high cost in which an egregiously expensive steel supply plays a central role — which together with poor design is making it increasingly difficult to sell goods abroad and increasingly profitable or agreeable to supply ourselves from foreign sources. While our foreign aid and assistance help create exports, it is also the difference between large exports and more modest imports which we use to help other countries. The prices of our products — in particular the prices in heavy industry — have now become more important than their quantity. Our ability to produce a surplus for export is unimportant if it is too costly for others to buy.

So even though we may wish for a more rapid and reliable economic growth for other reasons, a production contest with the Soviets will not much advance our cause. Without further action it would not supply the goods to the people who most need more. It would add nothing in itself to our military or economic power. And it could divert attention from more important things.

4

The objectives of the competition with the Soviets — the things which score on the board — are most vividly illuminated by the Sputniks and the lunar probes. To contemplate these for a moment is to see the true nature of the competition.

Coupled no doubt with the military threat, but by no means dependent on it, these achievements added enormously to the Soviet prestige. They modified the world-wide tendency — a tendency by no means confined to the non-Communist lands — to assume that such achievements come normally from the United States. A myth of American scientific omnipotence was dispelled. But scientific achievement has long been a source of national prestige. In Germany, France, Britain, the United States — notably also in Czarist Russia — scientific accomplishment has been a major source of national renown. In a day when science is so closely allied not only with military power but also health, physical well-being, and economic advance, it is natural that scientific prowess should be a special source of esteem. One may add that the Russians have also hit upon a form of scientific achievement with a unique capacity for advertising itself.

What the space exploration has shown is the vitality and vigor and cultural dynamism in one important dimension of Soviet society. It is this which has impressed the other people of the world, including ourselves. The Soviets have also been careful to moderate the military threat implicit in their achievement. This threat also is impressive but at the price of giving a warlike overtone to the accomplishment, which detracts from the image of the boldly scientific society. The Soviets have seen that to impress, they should not unduly frighten.

If we take the Soviet success as our guide, the competition is in those things which reveal the quality and effectiveness of the social order and hence its attraction to, and repute among, the varied inhabitants of the globe. It is not a purely scientific contest. Anything which manifests the quality of the society is important in the competition as so defined. Any weakness is damaging. The society with the most points of vitality and strength and the fewest of weakness will command the most respect and support. It will, one assumes, have the better chance of surviving. This, one further assumes, is the object of the race.

5

So to define matters is to see with some clarity our problems in the race and also our possible courses of action. We see again how barren the production race is — at least for us. It would add to our well-being. We should have more luxuries than before. But the rest of the world — including Russia — is already impressed by how well in general we live. Indeed we have already made too much of the American standard of living as a mark of our virtue. Consumption, conspicuous and otherwise, has always had its greatest appeal to the consumer.

We ought not assume that the competition is confined to space mechanics, as we show some signs of doing. Certainly our performance here should be far better than it has been. To the outside observer, at least, the effort seems to have consisted of a nearly unique combination of lethargy, bureaucratic rivalry, and *ex post facto* apology. We must determine to be the first to put a man in space, and it should be a public relations expert. But to confine our attention to space exploration is to limit ourselves to only one part of the competition and to a part where we are doing badly. It is, in effect, to allow the Soviets to confine the race to the things in which they have an advantage.

Above all, we must not assume that because the Soviets have a planned society and we, in general, do not, our rules preclude a planned response to Soviet initiatives. There is a dangerous tendency to imagine that faith in a free society means faith that it will accomplish everything that is needful without effort or direction. Or at most, incantation is all that is required. The effect of such a doctrine — a ruling doctrine in recent years — is to exclude an effective response to Soviet competition on grounds of principle. It means that we must fail because to succeed would be in violation of our ideology. For, in fact, most of the things which effective competition requires will also require effective government leadership. There is no alternative.

6

The indispensability of vigorous public leadership is evident when we consider the specific areas of competitive action. As noted, these consist of correcting manifest weaknesses in our social order and being aware of, and buttressing, our points of strength. Apart from the problem of race relations, of the importance of which we are on the whole aware, there are three weaknesses of our society which are gravely damaging to our reputation and prestige in the world at large and which cast a dark reflection on the quality of our society.

The first of these is the unhinged and disorderly quality of our urban society and the consequent squalor, delinquency, and crime. These are part of our world reputation for the usual reason that they are well observed by ourselves. We speak much of them and we are taken at our word. Hence the unpleasant image of violence and degradation which spreads around the world.

This is not the place for detailed diagnosis or detailed prescription, but on one thing we should be clear. This is a problem of American cities as it is not of Swedish, Dutch, German, or English cities. And it is not our problem because Americans are inherently more wicked than Swedes, Dutchmen, Germans or Englishmen. It is because we have given far less attention to the development and improvement of the urban community than have the European countries. The management of the European city is an opportunity not without its cultural and artistic responsibilities and rewards. Government in the American city remains a residual function — it does what the individual cannot do for himself, and not all of that. When a city administration is regarded as a necessary evil, we should not be surprised if it is evil.

Unemployment is the second great advertisement of inadequacy. It is especially important for it lends support to the Marxian contention that capitalism cannot function with its industrial reserve army. The traveler in the Communist lands and elsewhere finds that any explanation that he offers of unemployment in the United States is regarded as an apology — as, indeed, in some degree it is. We have developed over the years a remarkably sophisticated defense of a moderate amount of unemployment. Like the voice of a man shouting down the well, it is overpowering to the listener. But to others the beneficence of the recurrent recession is less evident. The fact that unemployment afflicts only a minority suffers somewhat from the fact that for that minority it is still a major misfortune. This is one of the instances where the man of sophistication is rendered helpless by the terrible tendency of people to remain obstinately with the unanswerable questions — in this case: Why shouldn't there be work for people who want to work?

To reconcile such opportunity with growth and reasonable stability of prices will also require public leadership.[2]

A third weakness — actual or presumed — is the role of arms expenditures in our economic life. There is a profound conviction, perhaps only a little less deep in the United States than abroad, that our economic system is sustained only by massive outlays by the Pentagon. Remove this buttress and we would have a disastrous collapse. The point is reinforced, on occasion, by the violent movements in the stock market when there is talk of disarmament — or alternatively of heightened tension. And while the Soviets spend heavily on arms, they have managed to avoid the suspicion that this is essential to their well-being. (Perhaps it is because they have no stock market.) Those who believe that the free economy can meet and master any contingency, and that nothing helps that tendency so much as their say-

---

[2] The requirements are discussed below, pp. 63 to 76.

ing so regularly, assure us (and the Russians) that a drastic reduction in arms outlays would involve no problems. The visit by Premier Khrushchev in the autumn of 1959 brought a virtual explosion of such utterances. They carried no conviction, for, unhappily, unction even when buttressed by pomposity is not a good substitute for evidence.

So our economy is thought to prosper only by the manufacture of instruments of destruction. Such an economy is unlikely to enjoy high prestige in the world; it is far more likely to repel than to attract. Yet that is our situation.

In my view we are not economically dependent on arms orders. (The politics of arms production may be more complex and serious.) Were peace to come this year or next, and were it possible to reduce our armed services to strictly ceremonial dimensions — even a ceremonial Army and Navy would now, no doubt, be very costly — we could readily replace the income so lost and the economic activity so given up. Reduced taxes on the lower income (and hence assured spending) brackets would offset a part of the loss. The backlog of public needs is massive, the equivalent, in some respects, of the accumulated personal needs after World War II. Reduction in the work week and increases in vacation time would require more workers for a given output. In particular industries and parts of the country — in the defense industries in the Los Angeles area, for example — the problem would be more serious. Part of the saving in arms outlays should be used for generous unemployment compensation for workers and severance pay for technicians, engineers and executives, and more of it might be used for grants to the cities that are specially affected. We could not make this transition without careful planning. But with

planning, and aided by the accumulated consumer demand
of the war years, we made a much greater transition between 1945 and 1947. Then the reduction in arms spending
was from $80.5 billion to $14.7 billion. Prices were about
half as high as now. So the real reduction was about three
times the present total defense expenditure of approximately
$46 billion.

We should map out — carefully and in detail — the course
of action to be followed in the event of reduced arms spending. The existence of a clearly specified alternative to arms
expenditures would show that we are not bound to this
dismal industry. This would add notably to the respect and
prestige accorded our economic system, both at home and
abroad. It might also keep the stock market from falling
when there is hopeful news on man's prospects.

7

The matters just mentioned — crime and disorder, unemployment, the seeming dependence on arms — weaken our
reputation in the eyes of our own people and in the eyes
of the world. They detract from the impression of quality
given by our society.

Yet it would be a great mistake to think of the competition in negative terms — as purely a matter of remedying
weaknesses, important as this may be. There is merit in the
redeemed sinner. But the heavenly officers who pass on his
redemption are men of affirmative virtue.

Without doubt the most important way of showing affirmative virtue is to have a strong and positive program of
assistance to the less fortunate lands. This is not an automatic by-product of domestic economic growth and expan-

sion; we can quite well consume all of our own output in the absence of a decision to use some of it for assistance to other people. Over the last two decades we have decided so to use some resources and we have reaped rich rewards from this decision. Critics of foreign aid might imagine what our present position in the world would be if we had been content since World War II to invest in our own comfort and well-being and let the rest of the world go by. One of the things now reasonably well established in international relations is the obligation of the richer countries to help the less fortunate lands. Historians will give us credit for this.

But in failing to see foreign aid as a manifestation of the quality of the society — as an index of its generosity and compassion and hence of its right to respect — we have severely damaged its usefulness. Ignorant and shortsighted men have regularly insisted on presenting it as a purely selfish thing. "I had one guiding principle in my conduct of ICA affairs," John B. Hollister, a former foreign aid administrator, said not long after leaving office. "Each proposed project had to be tested by a single standard: 'Will the spending of money for this purpose increase the security of the United States?' . . . my sole concern was and is the self-interest of this nation." [3]

This is slander. We have provided foreign aid mostly because we felt it was generous and right and perhaps a little out of a sense of guilt that we should be so well off while others were not. By such proclamations, we tell those who receive our help that they must consider themselves pawns in

[3] *Saturday Evening Post,* March 28, 1959.

our game. No man wishes to be a pawn. The total consequence is gravely to impair the usefulness of the aid in the
competition it is assumed to advance.

If we see the aid as a manifestation of the quality of our
society, we will also see that it does not advertise an expe-
dient or parochial attachment to the goals of the good
society. This happens when we extend assistance to corrupt
tyrannies or reactionary ruling oligarchies which are a principal menace to their own people. This also is regularly defended as the strategic course by the tough-minded and
hard-headed men. We have seen recently in Venezuela and
Cuba — as we shall see one of these days in the Dominican
Republic — how deep is the mistrust and how great the later
difficulty from such a course. Nor are the consequences
confined to the countries in question. When we support
tyrants and rascals, we everywhere support the impression
that we are indifferent to liberty, decency, and social justice.
This also we must not do. The proper and the practical
courses coincide.

8

Were the Soviets to press far ahead of us in some important
field of medicine or agricultural science — even in automobile propulsion — there would be more of the soul-searching
to which we are becoming so accustomed. That is because
we do not appreciate our advantages — and the prestige that
resides therein — until they are threatened. Where there is
no immediate challenge, we are inclined to imagine that
there is no competition.

The lesson would seem to be reasonably clear. In science

we should give at least equal attention to those fields where we are ahead and those where we are behind. Perhaps we should have some sort of regular scientific inventory to ascertain where — though ahead — we are slipping. As things now stand, or so it appears, we become aware of inadequate progress only when it puts us in second place.

But the problem of protecting and also using our advantage is not alone and perhaps not peculiarly confined to science. The scientific virtuosity of a society is only one measure of its quality. Other forms of intellectual and artistic achievement are also important. And they derive even more importance from the fact that it is the intellectuals and the artists who have both the first words and the last on the quality of a culture.

We should not be too superior about modern Soviet culture. The cultural life of the great Soviet cities is intense, professional, and interesting. Music, classical ballet, and the traditional stage are all excellent and enthusiastically supported. If some great novels get suppressed, some rather good ones now get published. The universities are large, well attended, and well equipped. The intellectual is a person of prestige. Yet in this part of life — especially in writing, the modern theater, painting, and architecture — our lead over the Soviets is great. And our advantage lies not in superior aptitude but in superior social context. The arts, to state a proposition of no breathtaking novelty, do not flourish where they are inhibited by formal dogma.

The world accords New York the honor and prestige of regarding it as a world capital, not because of the quality of our soldiers or our scientists or our statesmen, but because of the quality of our actors, playwrights, composers, artists, and architects. (The banality of Soviet painting and architecture is one of the most damaging advertisements of Soviet society.) The Soviet universities are large but they are far less varied and interesting than ours. It is with the better of ours, as with Oxford, Cambridge, and the University of Paris, that the intellectual community of the world tends to identify itself. This is no small advantage.

Yet it is an advantage that, on the whole, we ignore. When Premier Khrushchev visited the United States, he was shown a great many politicians, including some who do not especially commend themselves to the American people and a few who bear the concise designation of crummy. He saw some distinguished entrepreneurs and quite a few who are merely impressive. He saw shrunken ornamental shrubs at Beltsville and big corn in Iowa. He also saw Perle Mesta's machine shop. All of these exhibits, apart perhaps from the politicians, may have been marginally more remarkable than anything he could have seen in Russia. But the difference is only one of degree.

By contrast, he met no writers or artists. He did not see the Museum of Modern Art or the Whitney Museum — or even the new Guggenheim Museum. His glimpse of our contemporary architecture was incidental. He missed Tennessee Williams, Arthur Miller, and Rodgers and Hammerstein. He saw no great libraries. He saw little of our universities and nothing of their members. Perhaps Mr. Khrushchev wasn't interested. And perhaps in this instance nothing could be done. But the omissions are symbolic. It is by these things, far more than by our technical virtuosity, that we earn the respect and affection of the world — including, as the visitor there discovers, that of an astonishing number of Russians.

9

I would not wish to suggest that our competition with the Soviets is in any way frivolous or soft — it may be a measure of our miscalculation on cultural matters that it is necessary to say that competition in this sphere is not. But given our genius for self-interest both enlightened and otherwise, we must be on guard against proposals put forward in the name of competition by those who would find them convenient. During Mr. Khrushchev's visit, a large advertising agency took space in the New York papers to claim that more and better advertising was our secret weapon. In the months and years ahead, we will certainly be told that our superiority turns on better filter tips, the preservation of highway billboards, resistance to pay television, and the consumption of more aged whiskey. We should treat this idiocy with the contempt that it deserves.

But in a competition to develop and reveal the quality of our society, we must not rely on the wisdom of the solemn men. They will tell us that this is no time for reform — that, as always, other things are more urgent. They will do the Russians the honor of assuming that the only form of intellectual competition is in space exploration where the Russians are ahead. They will fail to see that our greatest achievements are those that depend on our capacity for economic and social experiment and change, and on the diversity and freedom of our culture.

Finally they will hope that the bill for doing what we must can somehow be avoided. Let there be no mistake. Most of the things we must do to reveal the quality of our society will cost money — public money. Willingness both to advocate and to pay is the test of whether a man is serious. If we haven't yet learned to mistrust, indeed to ignore, the man who talks about high national purposes and then omits all mention of the price — or perhaps urges strict economy in public outlays as one of his higher purposes — our case could be pretty bad.

II

The Decline of the Machine

THOSE WHO GUIDE our worries on large issues regularly ask us to ponder man's losing competition with the machine. On the assembly lines he is being replaced by automatic machinery which is regulated and instructed by electronic controls. If the resulting product is a consumer item it has almost certainly been designed to minimize both the effort and intelligence required of its user. Not even the question of whether people will want it has been left entirely to judgment. This has been ascertained by market surveys and insured by advertising and both, perhaps, were analyzed with the aid of an electronic computer, sometimes too ambitiously called an electronic brain.

The tendency to dispense with men and intelligence is held to go far beyond the consumer gadgets. The unmanned missile is about to replace the old-fashioned hand-operated bomber. In the near future, according to enthusiasts, unmanned missiles will take flight to intercept other unmanned missiles which will prevent these from intercepting other automated missiles. The operation will be handled under contract by IBM. If the globe were larger or the explosions smaller the prospect would be not unattractive. The machines having taken over, men would all be noncombatants.

The charm of war has always been greatest for those whose role was to guide it from a certain distance.

These visions of the triumph of the machine can be multiplied endlessly. We do not take them quite seriously for we do not really believe that we are being replaced, and our instinct is sound. If there is a competition between man and machine, man is winning it — not for at least two centuries has his position been so strong as compared with the apparatus with which he works.

And the fact that this is the age of ascendant man, not triumphant machine, has practical consequences. If machines are the decisive thing, then the social arrangements by which we increase our physical plant and equipment will be of first importance. But if it is men that count, then our first concern must be with arrangements for conserving and developing personal talents. It will be these on which progress will depend. Should it happen, moreover, that for reasons of antiquated design our society does well in supplying itself with machines and badly in providing itself with highly improved manpower, there would be cause for concern. There is such cause, for that, precisely, is our situation.

But first, what is the evidence that men have been gaining on machines — that skill and intelligence have become more important in what we call economic progress than capital plant and equipment?

2

The change is most prominently reflected in the changed position of the owner or supplier of physical capital. For a half century he has been a man of steadily declining prestige and importance. Once it was taken for granted that ownership of an industrial enterprise — the ownership of the capital assets or a substantial share of them — gave a man a decisive voice in its direction. So it was with Ford, Carnegie, the elder Rockefeller, Commodore Vanderbilt, and John Jacob Astor. And to be a source of capital, as in the case of the elder Morgan, insured an almost equal power over the enterprise. It also insured a considerable position in the community. Indeed, it was because the provision of capital conveyed such power that the system was called capitalism.

Now the ownership of capital, or the capacity to supply it, accords no such power. Few large corporations are now run by their owners; those like Du Pont where, for many generations, a talented family has had a decisive influence on the enterprise it owns, are becoming a rarity. Typically the power lies with the professional managers. These make elaborate obeisance to the stockholders. But they select the Board of Directors, which the stockholders then dutifully elect, and in equally solemn ritual the Board then selects the management that selected it. In some cases, for example the Standard Oil Company of New Jersey, once dominated by the first Rockefeller, the Board consists exclusively of managers selected by the managers who were selected by the Board.

There are a number of reasons for the rise of the professional manager, but by far the most important is that ownership of capital has come to count for much less than ownership of ability, knowledge, and brains. The man of ability could get the capital; the man who had capital and was

devoid of other qualification had become pretty much a
hopeless case. (Even to give away his money would eventually require the services of a professional.) The relatively
impecunious but better-trained, more intelligent, more determined, or politically more adept managers have almost
everywhere taken over. Once in office it is only rarely that
the owners of capital can dislodge them.

Nor is this a misfortune for the companies in question.
Some of the worst cases of corporate misfortune in recent
times have been those in which the owners of the capital
have managed to use their power to keep the professionals
out. In the thirties and early forties the elder Henry Ford
used his power as the sole owner of the Ford Motor Company to remain in command. It is now freely acknowledged
that the company suffered severely as a result. Following
his death the management was professionalized and much
improved. The great merchandising house of Montgomery
Ward under Sewell Avery provided a parallel example. Control and direction of a large company by a capitalist has
become, indeed, a rather risky affair. He may try to do what
can only be done well by a professionally qualified group
of diverse and specialized talent.

3

But though it is most visible at the top, the shift in the com-
parative importance of men and capital is perceptible
throughout the modern industrial enterprise. The procedures by which the large and successful enterprise raises
funds for new plant and equipment are orderly and predictable. And, depending on circumstances, there is a

considerable range of choice — earnings can be withheld, there can be resort to banks, or securities can be sold. A great deal of pompous ritual attends this process, but for the large and successful firm this signifies neither uncertainty nor difficulty but only that we have considerable respect for money and expect large sums to be handled with decent ceremony.

There is no similar certainty in the procedures by which even the most successful concern supplies itself with talent. It must send its emissaries to participate in the annual talent hunt, and if the most imposing men still go to the money markets, the most eloquent go to the colleges. The bag is always uncertain and frequently inadequate. If a successful firm is contemplating a considerable expansion it will almost certainly worry more about where to find the men than where to get the money.

And the change is reflected in the fears and apprehensions of the community at large. We wonder whether we are investing as much as we should in physical capital; we hear that the Soviets, who in our time have largely replaced conscience as the stern small voice of duty, are doing much more. But there is more everyday concern about the state of our schools and colleges. Are they doing properly by our children? Where can we find the resources to enable them to do better? Increasingly we are wondering about the adequacy of our output of highly trained and educated people.

This shows itself in a very practical way. Every family knows that the automobile industry is equipped to supply it with a new car almost on a moment's notice. Such is the admirable condition of our physical plant. But it cannot be at all sure there will be a place for all the children in a good college. Even the automobile executive may wonder where he can get his boy in. Such is the contrasting state of our facilities for human development.

4

The forces back of the change in the relative position of man as compared with capital are not new. Some of them, curiously enough, are those which, at first glance, seem to suggest the ascendancy of the machine.

The classical trinity of productive factors were land (including natural resources), labor (broadly defined to include both physical and intellectual effort), and capital. All production was seen as resulting from the combination of these factors in one form or another and in one proportion or another. Some economists have questioned whether there was much difference between land and capital goods — both support man's efforts to produce things, and many economists have insisted on adding as a fourth factor of production entrepreneurship or the human effort which was devoted to organizing and managing the other three factors. Subject to these modifications and a few quibbles, the classical delineation of productive agents is still accepted and, indeed, is deeply imbedded in economic thought.

All production requires all three (or all four) factors and in this sense all are equally vital. But the importance attached to the different factors has changed remarkably in the last hundred and fifty years. At the beginning of the last century — the formative years of modern economics —

land seemed peculiarly important. Population was growing. Europe and Asia seemed very crowded. The vast fertile spaces of the Americas, Australia, and Africa were but slightly appreciated. The effect of modern agricultural techniques on production per acre was, of course, beyond view. Both Ricardo and Malthus, two of the towering figures in the history of economic ideas, concluded that, in different ways, man's fate would be largely decided by the relentless pressure of population on limited land. Labor being abundant, perhaps excessively so, it seemed far less important than land. Capital, though important, also lacked the life-and-death significance of the land supply. Land was the factor of greatest prestige.

As the nineteenth century passed, capital gained rapidly to a position of dominance in the trinity. The new world added enormously to the supply of land. The decisive question was its development and for this ports, steamships, roads, railroads, farmsteads, and farm equipment were needed. The land was there; the labor came almost automatically; but the more capital the greater the pace of progress.

This emphasis on capital was reinforced by the nature of industrial advance during the last century. It consisted not of the invention of a great number of new techniques but the spread of a relatively small number of spectacularly important ones. Thus, textile manufacture became a factory industry. Steam power was applied to manufacturing, transport, and mining to replace power from men, animals, falling water, or wind. Iron and steel became plentiful and cheap and thus available for many new uses.

These inventions resulted, so far as anyone could tell, from a combination of accident, inspiration, and genius. Men like James Watt, Benjamin Franklin, and Eli Whitney could not be cultivated, and while they might under some circumstances be protected by the patent office, that was about all that could be done to foster technological progress.

But if little could be done to stimulate inventions, much could be done about putting them to use. Savings could be stimulated by exhortations to thrift — and even more by a system of ethics and religion which assured the diligent, abstemious, and self-denying man esteem in this world and salvation in the next. Investment could be encouraged by stable government and laws which assured investors that profits would be theirs to enjoy. Looking rationally at the thing that was subject to wise policy, economists came to measure progress by the proportion of the nation's income that, each year, was saved and invested.

5

Investment in physical capital is still a prime measure of progress but it is an obsolescent one. More and more progress is coming to depend on the quality rather than the quantity of the capital equipment in use and on the intelligence and skill of those who use it.

There are reasonably good figures to go on. Between the early seventies of the last century and the decade 1944–53, according to calculations made under the auspices of the National Bureau of Economic Research, the net output of the American economy increased by an average of 3.5 per cent a year. Less than half of this (1.7 per cent) is explained by increases in the supply of capital and labor.[1] The rest was the result of improvements in capital equipment — technological advance — and improvements in the working force, including, of course, its leadership and direction. The *share* in the advance attributable to technological improvement and to the improved skill and ability of workers, technicians, and managers has been increasing.

But both technological advance and improved skills and abilities are the product of personal development. Machines do not improve themselves; this is still the work of highly improved men. And most technological advance is now the result not of the accident of inspiration or genius but of highly purposeful effort. Once we had to wait for the accidental appearance of Edisons and Wrights. Now through education and organized effort in a laboratory or experimental shop we get something approaching the same results from much more common clay.

So it comes to this. We now get the larger part of our industrial growth not from more capital investment but from improvements in men and improvements brought about by highly improved men. And this process of technological advance has become fairly predictable. We get from men pretty much what we invest in them. So now in its turn, after land and after capital, labor — highly improved labor to be sure — has come to the center of the stage. Investment in personal development is therefore at least as useful as an index of progress as investment in physical capital. It

[1] These figures have been most thoughtfully interpreted by Professor Theodore Schultz to whom all who discuss these matters are in debt. See his "Investment in Man: An Economist's View," *Social Service Review*, XXXIII, No. 2, June 1959.

could be more valuable. This is the kind of change which solemn men of self-confessed soundness of judgment will continue to resist; the familiar is always defended with much more moral fervor just before it becomes foolish.

What then of our practical accommodation to this new urgency of investment in personal development?

6

At first glance our position would seem to be quite good. We have been reaping large gains from the application of trained intelligence to our economic life. This is the fruit of one of the world's pioneer experiments in public education. Surely our advantage will continue.

We cannot be so optimistic. Until the last century learning and even literacy were the badges of privilege. They had always been reserved to the favored few. Accordingly learning was a symbol of equality — a symbol that our grandparents, determined to establish their claim to full equality, were not disposed to overlook. Hence the free elementary schools, high schools, the Land Grant College system, and the remarkable number and variety of other institutions of higher (and not excessively high) learning.

This system was adequate, even admirable, so long as education was a socially provided service designed to insure (though it had other purposes too) rough equality of opportunity. It has ceased to be sufficient as education has become a form of investment.

The test of what a community should spend on a social service is what it can afford — what it believes it can spare from other forms of consumption. The test of investment,

by contrast, is what will pay for itself. We apply the investment test as a matter of course to physical capital and even
the commonplace terminology reflects the different attitudes;
while we "invest" in physical capital, we "spend" for education.

The investment test is far the more generous of the two
— that is to say, it sanctions much larger outlays. It implies
an aggressive canvass of all possible uses of funds to see
what will pay off at a profit. To find new ways of investing
at a profit is to prove one's enterprise. One of the most familiar theorems of accepted economics is that, subject to
some lags and irregularities, investment in physical capital
will occur whenever marginal return exceeds the marginal
cost; that is, whenever the return to additional investment
is sufficient to cover the added cost including interest and
some allowance for risk.

The test of what can be afforded, by contrast, invokes far
more frugal attitudes. The outlay, even if it is for education,
is vaguely self-indulgent. If we wish it — if we wish our
children to have the prestige and satisfactions and opportunities from learning — we must measure the cost against
other important alternatives. Virtue resides not in finding
ways of investing more but in finding ways of spending less.
The community honors the man who is identified with
economy. These attitudes remain even though, as we have
seen, the outlays economized may yield as large a return
(perhaps larger) as those for physical capital.

Investment in personal development is also handicapped
by the lack of a close relationship of outlay with the resulting benefit. A chemical company invests in a new plant

because it knows it will get the higher earnings. If it invests in the education of a young chemist it has no similar assurance that it will get a return from its outlay. The fellow may decide to become an artist or a farmer, or he may go faithlessly to work for a competitor.

One can see by a simple illustration what the kind of firm relationship of cost to benefit that exists for physical capital would do for investment in personal development if it existed there. Imagine an arrangement by which promising youngsters, when halfway through high school, were indentured for life to a corporation. The corporation would then be responsible for all further education and would be assured of their services for life. Performance of the companies tomorrow, it would soon be evident, would depend on the quality of the postulant executives, scientists, and other specialists being selected and trained today. The quality of this group would become a matter of major concern. It would be under the eye of accomplished educators. Money would start flowing into it. Investment fund managers would send scouts to seek information on its quality. If one of the larger oil companies found that the schools and colleges available for training its oncoming geologists and engineers were inadequate, it would obviously have to take steps to remedy the situation — perhaps by establishing its own. Otherwise, in a few years, it would be outclassed by the companies with better talent. One can easily imagine bond issues by backward companies to develop stronger technical echelons. The result would be a substantial and possibly an astronomical increase in outlays for personal development — all justified by the resulting profit. All this would be the result of giving the corporation a firm lien on the individual's services and thus on the return on the money it spends on him. It has such a lien on a machine; the example only makes human beings as privileged, for purposes of investment, as are machines.

The final reason for thinking that our arrangements for investing in personal development are deficient is that the Soviets have, technically speaking, superior ones. They begin with all resources under public control; hence, there is no problem in transferring those to be devoted to personal development from private to public use. And outlays for physical capital and those for personal development are items in the same huge budget. The returns from one type of investment can be measured against the returns from the other. There is no inherent reason why physical capital should have a preference as in our case. The result is that the U.S.S.R., by our standards still a comparatively poor country, treats its schools, research and training institutes, universities, and adult and worker education with a generosity which impresses all Western visitors. These outlays, needless to say, not old-fashioned expansion of physical capital, were decisive for launching the Sputniks and for landing their successor on the moon.

7

We cannot solve the problem of personal investment by indenturing our youngsters at a tender age to a corporation. And we should not expect the kindly corporation to rise to the rescue with large voluntary grants for education. Time has already been wasted on this notion. The problem is far too serious to be left to the conscience of those with a particular willingness to spend the stockholder's money.

Most likely we will solve the problem by making fuller and better use of the familiar instruments of public finance. We must see spending for personal development not as a cost but as an opportunity. Then we must make sure that we are taxing ourselves sufficiently to exploit this opportunity. That the Federal Government must play a role is elementary. It has access to fiscal resources that are inherently far greater than those of states and localities; now that education has become an investment rather than a social service, these resources are indispensable. It is also the unit of government with responsibility for national development and growth. There is at least a likelihood that investment in personal development is a better guarantee of national power than some of our military expenditures.[2]

We need also to review our attitudes toward state and local taxation. In a poor country there are sound reasons for reluctance in taxing objects of everyday consumption in order to have more public services and amenities. But we are not a poor country and personal development has become not a service but an investment. So states and localities should no longer hesitate to use sales and excise taxes (as an addition to and not as a substitute for others) to pay for schools and universities. And liberals, in particular, should not be too indignant when this is proposed.

There is another way of putting provision for personal

[2] We must see too that waste, including that of the athletic circuses, is brought under control. It is not only indefensible in itself; it brings investment in human development into disrepute.

development on a par with capital development that we should consider. We assume that a corporation, either by withholding from earnings or by resort to the capital market, will take responsibility for improving and expanding its own physical plant. The pressure for voluntary contributions by corporations to education reflects, no doubt, a feeling that there is a similar responsibility for personal development. Corporations are the largest employers of trained talent. They reap the rewards from employing such people. Why shouldn't they pay a part of the cost of training this talent?

Perhaps they should. Voluntary contributions will always be inequitable as well as inadequate. Conscience can readily be assuaged by a small contribution and the levy falls only on those with a social view of the corporation. But a special tax for education and training would encounter no similar objection. Levied as a percentage of total payroll — executive, scientific, skilled and unskilled — it would be roughly proportioned to the quantity and quality of the people employed. Thus it would be related to benefit from past investment in personal development; and it would mean that the company was assuming its rough share of the cost of replacing with improved talent the skilled workers, technicians, scientists, and executives that it employs. Initially the tax would presumably be borne in the form of higher prices by the consumers of the product. Ultimately the better talent would bring better methods, improved efficiency, and hence lower prices. It would be self-liquidating for it supports a profitable investment.

Corporations are now at great pains to explain that their

prices must include provision for earnings sufficient to replace and expand their physical capital. This, they regularly
assure their public, means that production will continue and
be more efficient in the future. But, as the National Bureau
figures show, we have more to gain from improving the
quality of people. So a levy for this purpose would be an
even better bargain.

Maybe there are other ways of augmenting the flow of
resources into personal development. In a society that is
changing we dare not assume that we have thought the last
thoughts on any such subject. For man has not retreated
before the machine; rather the machine has become desperately dependent on the improvement of man. And our
economy is still arranged to supply machines rather than
to improve men.

III

Economics and Art

This chapter began with a lecture invitation in the summer of 1959 from the New York Museum of Modern Art. I have an amateur's interest in painting and also in architecture and design. I have never been nearly as certain of the distinction between the good and the less good as most of my friends. This has made me subject to mild pity both by myself and others. But I have become persuaded that improving economic well-being requires an increasingly close relationship between the artist and economic life and that the price of alienation will be a disappointing and even frustrating banality in our society. So, with appropriate scholarly misgivings, I ventured on this unfamiliar task. I have been much helped and also a little reassured by my Harvard colleagues in the Department of Fine Arts and the School of Design and by members of the staff of the Museum. But they are nowise to be blamed for the result.

SEVERAL YEARS AGO at a leading eastern university the case arose of a young assistant professor of economics. He was an able and even brilliant teacher. He had written a number of good papers. One or two in particular showed originality, technical virtuosity and incomprehensibility, a combination which is held in the highest professional regard. But he had grave drawbacks. These included a passion for music and painting and a morbid lack of interest in the ordinary manifestations of material well-being. He lived in evident contentment in a small house heated by a coal stove. It was sensibly decided — though it must be said not without discussion — that he had no future as an economist. He was not promoted.

The incident illustrates the traditional relationship between art and economics. There is none. Art has nothing to do with the sterner preoccupations of the economist. The artist's values — his splendid and often splenetic insistence on the supremacy of aesthetic goals — are subversive of the straightforward materialist concerns of the economist. He makes the economist feel dull, routine, philistine, and uncomfortable and also sadly unappreciated for his earthy concern for bread and butter including that which nourishes the artist. Not only do the two worlds not meet, but the regret in each is evidently negligible.

This alienation, though unregretted, is unfortunate. The economist can perhaps say something useful to the artist about his environment and what nourishes the artistic imagination. And the artist stands in far more important relation to economics, and indirectly to politics, than we have yet realized. I will end this chapter by arguing that one of the more important problems of our day — the weakening of the American balance of international payments and the complex of foreign and domestic issues which follow in its train — is partly the result of the alienation of the artist from our economic life. But first a word or two of explanation.

The amateur venturing into the world of art is soon made to feel the perils of his path. Art is the creation of beauty and its language. But art and how to deal with Russia have this in common: that subjectivity is the parent of both certainty and emotion. One man's beauty, it is clear, is another man's missed opportunity; had the critics been present at the time, there would have been some highly deprecatory words about the Lord's creative instinct. I shall not venture to say what is beauty; and fortunately for the purposes of this chapter, I need only to be allowed a certain band within which it will be agreed that it occurs. Whether a particular artist or work belongs within this band is not something I need decide.

I have need to refer not only to the artist but to those for whom his language has meaning. This is the community which shares the artist's imagination and responds to it. Its size and the depth and discernment of its response are matters of much importance. I shall refer to it simply as the aesthetic response.

2

The economic myth of the artist is of the man devoid of material baggage and indifferent to pecuniary reward. It is not a myth that can be reconciled entirely with reality. In the Greco-Roman epoch, the painter or sculptor soiled his hands at a wearisome and hence unbecoming toil. Accordingly, and unlike the poet, he was identified with the artisan and the slave, and his pay was that of a worker.[1] This was only slightly less so of the early Renaissance artists — Hauser describes them as "economically on a footing with the petty bourgeois tradesman." [2] However, by the latter

[1] Arnold Hauser, *The Social History of Art* (New York: Alfred A. Knopf, 1951), Vol. 1, p. 124.
[2] Ibid., p. 315.

part of the fifteenth century, the great painters had, financially speaking, come into their own. Raphael and Titian lived handsomely on ample incomes. Michelangelo was a wealthy man; it was because of his wealth that he was able to decline payment for the design of St. Peter's. Leonardo ultimately received a handsome salary.

In later times it is difficult to make a rule. The Dutch masters, as a consequence of heavy overproduction, had a hard time. Rembrandt, Hals, and Vermeer led a financially precarious existence. For what we would now call reasons of economic security, van Goyen traded in tulips, Hobbema was a tax collector, and Jan Steen was an innkeeper. In modern times Van Gogh, Gauguin, and Toulouse-Lautrec were vagabonds because this was implicit in their alienation from bourgeois civilization. But interspersed through the history of Western painting from Rubens to Picasso have been others who have earned great fortunes. This has included Americans. Copley was rich enough to speculate in real estate and owned much of Beacon Hill. Winslow Homer lived a very comfortable life.[3] The most popular of the abstract expressionists are being handsomely rewarded by any standards. It is not clear that wealth, for the artist, has been or is an insuperable obstacle.

What is not in doubt is that the aesthetic response is nourished by secure well-being. From classical Athens through the princes, bankers and popes of the Renaissance, the Dutch bourgeois of the seventeenth century, the courtly patrons of the seventeenth and eighteenth centuries to the collectors and connoisseurs of modern times, wealth has been the unmistakable companion of art. Perhaps it has not

[3] Details for which I am indebted to my colleague, John Coolidge.

always brought a discerning interest. But if it has not been a sufficient, it certainly has been a facilitating influence. The artist may transcend hunger and privation — conceivably his senses are honed by his suffering. But not so his audience. It turns to art after it has had dinner. At first glance, such a philistine assertion will seem surely suspect. But, subject always to individual exceptions, it will hardly be argued that the aesthetic response has been as strong from the poor and the insecure as from the rich and established. "Great periods in art have traditionally come with stability in government, with prosperity and leisure." [4] "The overworked, driven person or class is seldom creative, while leisure, even wasteful leisure, may end creatively." [5]

3

One can bring these matters within the scope of a simple hypothesis. It is that pecuniary motivation — roughly the desire for money income — has a marked tendency to preempt the individual's emotions. Only as it releases its grip is there opportunity for artistic, or, for that matter, for any cultural or intellectual interest not immediately related to income. As Alfred Marshall observed, "the business by which a person earns his livelihood generally fills his thoughts during by far the greater part of those hours in which his mind is at its best." [6] If he and his family live under the threat of hunger, cold or exposure, this preoccupa-

---

[4] Edward Durrell Stone, "The Case Against the Tailfin Age," *New York Times*, October 18, 1959.

[5] Bernard Berenson, *One Year's Reading for Fun: 1942* (New York: Alfred A. Knopf, 1960), p. 93.

[6] *Principles of Economics* (London: Macmillan, 8th edition, 1927), p. 1.

tion will be total. By the same token, to remove the threat of physical hardship will be, other things equal, to weaken the role of pecuniary motivation and allow other influences to enter the pattern of life.

The fear of hardship, we may assume, will play somewhat the same pre-emptive role as hardship itself. And fear is not confined to physical hardship. As most people are constituted, they will be perturbed by any serious threat to existing levels of well-being. They defend accustomed living standards with considerable tenacity.[7] Accordingly, if people are so circumstanced that they live under the threat of a reduction in income — of being plunged into some dark and half-imagined abyss — pecuniary motivation will be strong. The gods are waiting to hurl the unwary man to his doom; they can only be propitiated by unremitting vigilance. The secure man, in contrast, can turn his thoughts to other matters.

Until comparatively recent times the preferred model of a nonsocialist society was one of marked uncertainty. Production was for a common market made by many sellers; in this market, prices moved freely in response to changes in consumer taste or need or changes in cost and output. Incomes, at least, in the form of profits, salaries or wages were inherently insecure.[8] Favorable profits, for example, would attract new participants. This was possible, for entry into any business was assumed to be inexpensive and easy.

[7] See the studies reported on and conclusions reached by Professor James S. Duesenberry in his *Income, Savings and the Theory of Consumer Behavior* (Cambridge: Harvard University Press, 1949), pp. 76 et. seq.

[8] The case of income accruing from rent is rather different. And it is proof of the point that the more secure and leisurely landlord has long been considered accessible by the artist.

The resulting increase in supply would lower prices and therewith profits, and, in practice, the uncoordinated response of numerous new entrants could easily cause profits to disappear. Profits could also disappear as the result of unexpected or inexplicable shifts in consumer taste or changes in technology which gave other producers a sudden and substantial advantage in cost. Wages and salaries shared the uncertainty of the income from which they came.

The uncertainty of this model, it should be noted, was not only intrinsic but a virtue. It was what punished sloth and kept producers on their toes. This is almost exactly to say that the system was designed to make pecuniary motivation as nearly pre-emptive as possible.[9] It was meant to be artistically barren, for it rewarded a full-time concern with making money and it drove its participants with the omnipresent possibility of failure.

The nearest approach to the competitive model in the American economy is agriculture. Here many comparatively small producers do supply a common market under conditions which, in the past at least, have been characterized by marked uncertainty. In this industry earnings often have suddenly and disastrously disappeared for many participants. Without stopping to consider the reason, we expect the modern practicing farmer to be beyond the reach of the aesthetic response. That the successful lawyer should have a concern for painting does not surprise us. But not the suc-

[9] It did not, of course, exclude religious motivation. But this is not in conflict with pecuniary motivation. It nowise interferes with the work week and, as in the case of Calvinism, it provides a moral sanction and reinforcement for economic achievement.

cessful cattleman. He is the man for whom the calendars and *The Saturday Evening Post* covers are drawn. As his income increases, he may develop an interest in a better automobile, possibly in an airplane and certainly in an array of consumers goods. That he should develop a serious concern for painting or sculpture or even for domestic architecture is not expected. A farmer has too many other worries. He cannot be frivolous or eccentric. Unlike the more secure lawyer, it is in fact taken for granted that his pecuniary concerns are pre-emptive.[10]

As with the farmer, so generally with the small businessman — the dealer, salesman, contractor, and small merchant. His income may be handsome by any past standards. But he is a man who has to hustle. Accordingly, the arts are not for him. George Babbitt, who in secret moments hungered for something with slightly more magic, knew in the end that he had to keep his thoughts on the real estate business. The competitive economy still imposes this requirement.

4

Were ours still an economy of insecure small producers, we would have therein a sufficient explanation of the alienation of art from economic life. The insecurity of such a society is pre-emptive; the aesthetic response will only be strong

[10] I am here characterizing an attitude. It is one to which, I would certainly assume, there are many individual exceptions. And one reason for wishing for a greater security of farm income is to enlarge the number of exceptions. That an increase in the amount and security of income should bring an artistic and cultural renaissance on the farms should not strike us as odd. That is what income is for. Yet even those who are at first moved to think all this an aspersion on the agrarian soul will think it odd.

where it is somehow protected from the dominant economic motivation.

But modern economic society does not conform to the competitive model. The centerpiece of the modern capitalist economy is the great corporation. It is an institution which is arranged to provide a rather large number of people rather large and secure incomes. Through control of its prices and of its sources of supply, by diversification of its products, by research which insures that technological innovation does not catch it unawares and, in degree, by the management of consumer tastes, the modern corporation has either eliminated or much reduced the main sources of insecurity of the competitive firm. Consequently earnings are highly reliable; of the one hundred largest industrial firms in the United States, not one failed to earn a profit in 1957, and this was a year of mild recession.[11]

As a result the modern corporate executive enjoys a security of income and tenure comparable with that of a college professor. In examining the protection which a vocation accords to the individual, one should examine the fate not of the successful but of the unsuccessful. The benign and protective character of government employment is indicated by the decorative sinecures into which the inadequate can be sidetracked with appropriate ceremony. Ambassadorships in untroubled countries, assistant secretaryships for public affairs or membership on the Federal Communications Commission are all available. In colleges and

---

[11] *Fortune*, August, 1958. (Of the largest two hundred, only one, an automobile manufacturer, failed to turn in a profit. Size is here measured by volume of sales.)

universities, compassion is similarly manifested by establishing research projects for reviewing progress in behavioral sciences or international relations, by appointments as deans for relations with parents, wives, or the local churches or to committees to reconsider the curriculum. But the modern corporation is peculiarly rich in its arrangements for cushioning the fall of the man who stumbles in mid-career. Not only are a wide variety of posts — public relations, staff relations, community liaison, charitable contributions, supervision of office festivities — available with honorific titles, but there is also in most firms an understanding not present in the university that all will deny fiercely that any featherbedding is involved.

Accordingly, the comparatively secure and remunerative life provided by the modern corporation should be hospitable to the arts. Eventually it will be — and for the good of the economy, it must so become. However, the myth of the insecure, tough, competitive enterprise has outlasted the reality. Business is assumed still to require a total concentration of energies; anything less is still deemed to be out of character. And men are still treated by their commitment, or their simulation of a commitment, to what is held to be a demanding, no-nonsense, nose-to-the-grindstone, hard-driving existence. To suppose that the requirements of a business career are secondary, or supplementary, to artistic or cultural interests or a means of supporting them is still the exception. There are distinguished exceptions, but they depart from the general rule. At the turn of the century, Charles Lang Freer made his business, as a builder of railroad cars, the servant of his interest in Whistler and

Oriental art. His industrialist friends complained that he preferred talking about the tariff on paintings to discussing the price of steel.[12] Such talk might still cause question about his effectiveness as a businessman.

Indeed one senses that there has even been a partial reversal of form. Two generations ago, with the highly interested assistance of Duveen, the great tycoons proved by their art collections that they were not mere money-grubbers. A few million dollars invested in Botticelli, Fra Angelico, Rembrandt, or Vermeer showed, as nothing else, that the investor was identified with the secure and aristocratic leisured classes from the Renaissance on. Now the organization man may seek to prove the opposite. In his single-minded devotion to his enterprise, he shows that he is identified in spirit with the hard-bitten entrepreneurship but not the other interests of Henry Clay Frick, Andrew Mellon, and J. Pierpont Morgan.

Modern Soviet painting — the socialist realism which depicts strong maidens looking over the high-yielding wheat to the sun — asserts that art is the handmaiden of economics. Its goal is to help organize the country for the maximum of aesthetically static output. Those who insist on the total primacy of economic motivation in our economic life come out at curiously near the same point. They too are likely to insist on forthright realism — and defend it, not without indignation, as "what the people want." They may also, on occasion, be suspicious of what unduly taxes the imagination. The precise painting which official Communist critics

[12] Aline Saarinen, *The Proud Possessors* (New York: Random House, 1958), p. 125.

characterize as bourgeois degeneracy, the down-to-earth American conservative condemns as Communist-inspired. Both, we may imagine, find it difficult to reconcile such art with pre-emptive pecuniary motivation. Although the need to defend this no longer exists, the habit persists.

5

To the extent that the business firm still insists on the primacy and inviolability of artistic goals, it excludes and alienates the artist and narrows the aesthetic response normal to a society of secure well-being. There are three other ways in which the model of a competitive society, as it affects its corporate successor, is at odds with the artist. One of these, of particular importance to the architect, is its tendency to deny him control of the aesthetic environment. In the competitive model, the role of the state is slight. It is meant to be a self-regulating economic society in which the best government, in economic matters, governs the least. The modern corporate economy has found it convenient to assert the same rule wherever it is reasonably plausible, for it keeps public authority from intruding on the not unwelcome exercise of private authority. In the years following World War II, and partly no doubt as reaction to the wartime controls and the individuals who administered them, we had a strong reaction against anything seeming to smack of centralized guidance of economic activity. Planning became an evil word. The uncontrolled development of economic activity was justified not only on grounds of efficiency. It became a moral good.

In Cambridge, Massachusetts, near the banks of the

Charles, there are two buildings — an auditorium and a chapel — by Eero Saarinen. They are, one imagines, beautiful buildings, but no one can really know. For on one side is an early Norman apartment house and on the other a dingy and decayed four-story brick. In front is a parking lot filled with multicolored and rather dirty cars; behind are a candy factory, a fireproof storage warehouse, and a large sign advertising the 57 Varieties. Down the road are purveyors of fried foods and gasoline. St. Mark's might well lose some of its charm were the Piazza San Marco surrounded by Gulf, Esso and Texaco stations, a Do-nut shop, with Howard Johnson's at the end. But such grotesque arrangements are strongly defended by the competitive ideology. They are the natural and valued consequence of competitive enterprise. The man who questions the outcome runs the risk of being called an impractical aesthete who has not properly grasped the principles which have made the system what it is today.

The second problem is advertising — not all of it but an important part. As people are less persuaded of their desires by physical need, someone is certain to seek to persuade them. The essence of this persuasion is to attract attention. This advertising does in one successful form by allowing beauty to attract our eyes or ears and then introducing a contrasting, which is to say, in practice, a jarring note. Thus advertising cannot seek harmony with its environment. The most beautiful billboards would be those that blended into the landscape — and were not seen. The most agreeable commercials would be those that did not interfere with the play or music — and were not heard. Such advertising, it will be contended, would be ineffective. But then it cannot be argued that the jarring alternatives are a contribution to beauty. In speaking of the pre-emptive tendencies of pecuniary motivation, I have been speaking of a force which alienates industry from the artist. Advertising — that which is juxtaposed to beauty — has the equal but opposite effect. It alienates the artist from industry. Possibly it is the most important influence determining the reaction of the artist to economic life.

Finally there is the conflict in which the modern industrial firm finds itself, under the best of circumstances, between the pursuit of sales and the pursuit of excellence. Few would wish to argue that the popular taste is the best taste, that it reflects the highest aesthetic response. And it is quite clear that the ordinary industrial firm must produce for the popular market. There may be thus, by the artist's standards, a deliberate preference for commonplace or banal design. But the businessman, in the first instance at least, is hardly to be blamed. When the Court and a few cultivated Parisians provided the principal market for French craftsmen, the standard of artistic excellence could be high. The standard would certainly have fallen if France had suddenly become a prosperous, egalitarian democracy.

However, it seems probable that modern industrial design has managed to get the worst of a bad bargain. Taste is not static. And change begins with those who are in communication with the artist — who have a strong aesthetic response. Industry, alienated from the artist and with its eyes fixed by way of the market researchers on the popular taste, has regularly failed to perceive those advances in taste which were rendering its designs banal and otiose. Instead of being a little ahead, it has been a little behind.

Progress toward better design has also been handicapped by planned obsolescence. To offset the excessive durability of products and the inhibiting effects of this on demand, many of them must be constantly restyled. These constant changes cannot but have an exhausting effect on the artistic resources of the industry. In the past, good design lasted for a long time — and this, one imagines, was one reason it was good.

6

In a diverse society such as ours, economic institutions are not coterminous with life; there is much room for development in the interstices. Accordingly, the pre-emptive role of economic motivation and the associated problems of the competitive society are not fatally damaging to the artist or to the aesthetic response. Certainly they are far less damaging than in the Communist countries.

We have seen, moreover, that part of the hostility — the determined preoccupation with down-to-earth pecuniary concerns in the modern large corporation — is based not on necessity but on the perpetuation of a myth. The myth is not invulnerable. Without question, its hold is weakening. Of all artists, the architect is the most dependent on the aesthetic response. Its absence brings us an enormous amount of very bad building with which, no doubt, we will have to put up for a very long time. The glass beehives and shoddy metal boxes which disfigure Manhattan, long our proudest architectural exhibit, are perhaps the greatest tragedy. But even here there are brilliant exceptions, although — if there is need to prove a rule — they have been mostly cases where, fortuitously or otherwise, pecuniary motivation was not predominant. Rockefeller Center was built by a noted affluent family of marked aesthetic response and at least partly as a demonstration piece. In the United Nations group, commercial motivations were absent and the architects had an exceptionally free hand. The Lever Brothers Building was built by a company headed by an architect temporarily miscast as a businessman. The Seagram Building no doubt reflects the greater need of a distillery for ultimate distinction than for immediate gain, and also the sensitivity of an influential daughter to the work of Mies van der Rohe. And there are many instances — the General Motors Technical Center, Connecticut General's new building and others — where corporations in the ordinary course of business have given rein to the artistic imagination.

It is not the artist who has suffered from the alienation of art from economics but the reverse. For the economic system the alienation is serious, more serious certainly than is imagined. In recent years there has been a sharp decline in the export of American goods. There had been an even more dramatic increase in the import of European-made products. As one result, the American balance of payments is weak — a brief episode in 1932–33 apart — for the first time in our modern history. In largest part the problem is one of cost; for a considerable range of our goods, we have been pricing ourselves out of world markets including our own. But in no small measure it is a matter of design; our goods have fallen below both European standards and our own tastes. Edward Durrell Stone observed not long ago that "the American people can afford everything but beauty." [13] But, in fact, they have been searching for it with no small diligence. And they have been finding it in Italian, French, German, and Swedish products far more than in their own. The automobile is the most important and also the most publicized example. But in a host of other products — furniture, glass, ceramics, leather, metalware — Americans have turned to foreign designs as foreigners have turned away from American products. And as Stone has also pointed out, in their search for beauty, our people have been turning away from the disorderly and billboard-studded American scene. This lies behind part of the annual tourist migration which also has an effect on the balance of payments.

Our failure has not been general. There is much good American design. Industry in many fields has come into communication with the artist — it has shown itself capable of a strong aesthetic response. But in an alarming number of instances this, clearly, is not the case. In these industries it is supposed that industry is something apart from art, or, at best, that the artistic imagination must be kept carefully subordinate to popular appeal. And here the customers have been responding to the closer identification of the European industry with the artist and vice versa, and the superior product that results.

That design is one dimension of quality no one will question. But that it is a dimension of growing importance must still be stressed. A poor society may ask only that its products

[13] Op. cit.

be well engineered. But a richer one is certain to require that they have beauty as well. In the earlier stages of industrialization the engineer is important. In the later stages he yields place to the artist. The practical man who holds that this is a lot of precious nonsense may, like the automobile makers, have to learn the truth the hard and expensive way.

Indeed one already senses that the learning is causing pain. One senses a kind of angry impatience over the rejection of various of our own products and the popularity of European replacements. This is something that is being put over by the highbrows and the cultural snobs. If the honest American had been left alone he would have remained with his honest chrome. We are a brass-rail-and-cuspidor folk; we welcome a nice dashboard, and a fancy decanter for our grain neutral spirits. The mark of an American is that he rises above any precious tendencies to look for beauty especially in useful things. There is not much future in this kind of cultural protectionism. Self-criticism will probably stand us in better stead.

7

To summarize, then: in a simple society, pecuniary motivation can be powerful and indeed transcendent. And perhaps it must be, for the earning of bread, where bread is scarce, has to be a preoccupying concern. But one of the happy consequences of security and reasonable well-being is that people have time and thought and emotion for other things. Economic institutions must in turn be responsive to this change. At least partly under the influence of the earlier myth, our institutions are less responsive than they should be. We are still reluctant, moreover, to accept the social and political arrangements, notably the planning, which would allow harmony between the artist and his environment. We are tolerant of the destruction of beauty if it sells the goods. Those who assail our senses or disfigure our land-scape for commercial purposes can still presume to claim that they are serving the paramount goal of the society.

The artistic imagination enters only rather furtively into economic life. Artistic truth is still revealed not by the artist but by the market researcher. In a community of developing taste, he may be a guide only to the obsolescent.

The remedies are not simple. Pecuniary goals are un-equivocal and direct. To avow and pursue them is an uncomplicated matter. To create beauty is anything but simple. The goals are highly equivocal — indeed it will regularly precipitate an awkward struggle over the nature of beauty. To recognize, as now we must, that society must assume responsibility for the protection of the aesthetic standards of the environment will bring bitter debate. So will the need to subordinate jarring salesmanship to aes-thetic goals. And the American businessman, having ac-commodated himself to the scientist in the course of ac-commodating himself to the twentieth century, must now come to terms with the artist. Artistic perception is as necessary to the modern manufacturer of consumers goods as engineering skill. Indeed now more so. How it is brought to bear is another and long story. But as a start, we can reject the myth that still holds that it has no place.

IV

Inflation: What It Takes

D URING the last two or three years, there has been an increasing measure of agreement on the causes of inflation and for that reason, one hopes, on the logic of the remedies. Evasion of the awkward questions is still possible and much practiced. But the hard core of the problem is obtruding itself.

This visible and inescapable core can be described briefly. And on a matter where words are frequently used to obscure meaning, there is considerable advantage in being brief. The purpose of this chapter is to give the essentials of the problem and its remedies in as few words as possible.

2

The primary economic and political condition which controls all useful discussion of price stability is the overriding importance of high employment. The opportunity for a job and the income that goes with it dominates our thinking on economic policy. And this is understandable. Unemployment is rarely considered desirable or healthy except by those who have not experienced it. For many, it remains the major misfortune of our society. One day we shall remove the economic penalties and also the social stigma associated with involuntary unemployment. This will make the economy much easier to manage. But we haven't done this yet.

High employment is also necessary for economic growth. High output — capacity operations — are an inducement to investment. Low output and idle plant capacity reduce the incentive to investment. Investment is what nurtures growth.

It follows from the foregoing that no policy designed to promote the stabilization of prices has any chance of permanent success if it depends, either directly or indirectly, on deliberately continued unemployment. Those who recommend such policies often get a certain amount of applause for the old-fashioned soundness of their views and for their courage in committing other people to misfortune. This should not be confused with popular approval.

Next we must be clear that, at high employment, prices in the American economy — or more particularly in one sector of it — are not stable. Defects exist in the design of economic systems as they exist in machines, or in the character and personality of statesmen. There is such a defect in our system. We do not remove it either by pretending that the defect doesn't exist or by horrified denunciation of those who point it out.

In that sector of the economy where firms are large and the control over prices by individual firms is substantial, there is opportunity for large discretionary increases in prices whenever demand is favorable. The demand that is favorable to high employment is favorable to such price increases. There is, moreover, a powerful incentive to exploit this price discretion when wages are raised. The cost of the wage settlement can then be passed to the public. So increases in wages are usually covered by a price increase — typically with something more. So long as demand is at, or near, full employment levels, we must expect that, in industries characterized by strong firms and unions, prices and wages will react on each other in a steady upward spiral. Even with considerable idle capacity, the spiral will continue in some industries.

The large and important commodity price increases in this decade have been those in steel, steel products, machinery, automobiles, pulp and paper, rubber, tobacco, and beverages. These, in general, are industries of few firms — the concentrated industries. Prices of textiles and apparel and most importantly of food have contributed little or not at all to the inflation. When the index has been stable in recent years, it has been not because of stability in the concentrated industries but because of the offsetting effect of falling prices in the unconcentrated or "competitive" industries.[1]

The role of steel in recent price inflation is of particular importance. "If steel prices had behaved *like other industrial prices*, the total wholesale price index would have risen by 40 per cent less over the last decade and less by 52 per cent since 1953. Finished-goods prices would have risen less by 23 and 38 per cent respectively." [2]

---

[1] Prices of services have also risen. This, however, is explained by the low rate of productivity gains in most service industries and the need to match, at least in part, the increase in money wages in the economy as a whole.

[2] From Otto Eckstein and Gary Fromm, *Steel and the Postwar Inflation* (Joint Economic Committee. Washington: 1959), p. 34. Italics added. The reference to the last decade is to the period 1949–1959.

3

The remedies for the inflation as just described follow with a certain obstinacy from the diagnosis. The possible courses of action, remedial or otherwise, are as follows:

1) Do nothing.
2) Rely on so-called monetary or fiscal measures or a combination of the two.
3) Break up the large corporations and unions.
4) Keep wage- and price-setting in the concentrated industries, such as steel, from being inflationary.

4

To do nothing is, of course, to accept the inflation. There are few forthright supporters of this position. There are many indirect or unconscious advocates who get to this position by opposing all available courses of action or who confine their intervention to prayer, incantation, and admonition.

To do nothing is not a tolerable choice. Let us reflect well on the kind of inflation we are talking about. It is led by the prices of the largest and strongest firms. It is paced by the wages of the largest and strongest unions. Those who lag, relatively or absolutely, are the weaker firms and weaker unions. Also the public servants, school teachers, unorganized workers, and others who do not have effective bargaining power. Also the retired and the aged who have no real bargaining position at all. Those who endorse an inflation of the modern sort are endorsing a policy of giving the most to the biggest and strongest and the least to the smallest and weakest. This is not the whole case against this inflation. It breaks faith with those who save. It is damaging to public services. It rewards not the most gifted people but the most gifted money-makers. It has had a devastating effect on our exports and it has greatly and unnaturally stimulated imports. The consequence has been a serious and possibly alarming deterioration in our balance of payments. But one point above all must be seen with clarity. The modern inflation is not neutral. Because of its inevitable identification with economic strength, it is inequitable, regressive, and reactionary.

5

Monetary policy is the effort to influence the level of prices by action of the central bank — in our case the Federal Reserve System. Fiscal policy is the effort to influence it by way of the budget — by having at some times an excess of public revenues over outlays which reduces total demand in the economy, and at other times an excess of expenditure over revenues which adds to demand. Neither monetary nor fiscal policy make contact with the present form of inflation in an effective and practical way. Firms in the concentrated sector of the economy can advance their prices, and do, whenever the economy is at or even near full capacity and employment. The level of use of capacity in an industry and the level of employment therein depend on the level of demand for goods in general and for the products of this industry as part of the general demand. Both monetary policy and fiscal policy make contact with the problem of inflation by reducing the general level of demand. To be effective, they must reduce demand enough to create idle capacity and unemployment since, to repeat, the price inflation occurs when these are not present in substantial amount. But a policy of creating idle capacity and unemployment collides with the higher objective of full employment and full use of capacity. As I have stressed, we set higher store by these than we do by price stability.

Let me add that monetary policy, under all circumstances, is a secondary instrument of public policy. Nothing is more salutary than our gradual discovery — more properly our gradual rediscovery — in these last few years that there is no subtle magic by which an economy can be guided and directed by the Federal Reserve. The less reliance we place on monetary policy, the better off we will be.

The case of fiscal policy is different. Although the purposeful use of taxes and expenditures to influence the level of economic activity will not of itself bring stable prices at full employment, fiscal policy is not, for that reason, unimportant. When there is unemployment and idle capacity, an excess of government expenditures over receipts is by far the surest way of expanding economic activity. Under such circumstances, we should have a budget deficit. And when output and employment are high, the budget should be balanced. Even though a balanced budget does not insure stability *at full employment*, it is one of the conditions necessary for stability at full employment. Budget balancing, one should add, does not necessarily mean reducing expenditures. If the services needed by the community exceed the revenues that the tax system yields at full employment, then the proper course is to raise taxes.

6

The position so far is this: at or near full employment we shall have inflation in the concentrated industries. Monetary and fiscal policy can cure this inflation only by severely cutting back demand and output and employment. This remedy is unacceptable because it is worse than the disease. The third possibility is to break up the large corporations and perhaps also the large unions. Let us, it is said, enforce the antitrust laws with all vigor and extend them somehow to the unions.

The antitrust laws serve a valuable purpose. They bring the conscience of the community to bear on the problem of economic power. They keep (or seek to keep) the strong firm from abusing its weaker customers, suppliers and competitors. For this reason, these laws have always had a strong claim on the interest of men of moral sense. They could, no doubt, be stronger and better enforced than they are.

But to suppose the antitrust laws will work the kind of revolution which would be necessary to reconcile full employment with price stability is out of the question. This would mean a wholesale revision in industrial structure including a wholesale break-up of existing business units. Even were this desirable, there is not the slightest indication from history that the antitrust laws, limited as they are by judicial process, can be the instrument for such a revolution.

Such a policy would also be politically divisive. Its application to unions would provide a field day for those who would think the attack on inflation a wonderful excuse for an attack on labor organization as such. The populist tradition may still nurture people who would be more attracted by the prospect of baiting corporations than stabilizing their prices.

There is no hope for an inflation remedy in the antitrust laws, new or old. To argue that there is may be to engender doubts about the effectiveness of the antitrust laws for other important purposes.

There have been somewhat similar proposals to cure this kind of inflation by eliminating all tariffs and exposing the industries that are raising their prices to the stern winds of international price competition. This suggestion is also of limited value. The winds of foreign competition may not be without a salutary impact on some industries, including steel. Inflation should not be protected by protection. But international competition does not operate effectively for many products, including those which are difficult or expensive to ship or which are wholly immobile. And the tariff is an old and politically rigid instrument. There is little practical chance that it could be used flexibly to force down prices. Those who offer such eye-catching proposals often confuse the sensation they create, which is large, with the practical consequence, which would be very small.

7

Only one course of action remains. That is some form of public intervention in that part of the economy where full employment, or an approach to full employment, means inflationary price and wage increases. Such intervention, when it comes, will not be the result of anyone advocating it. It will be because there are no practical alternatives.

Economists in considerable numbers are coming to accept the need for such intervention. A poll of professional economists conducted by the Joint Economic Committee of the Congress in 1958 showed that between 40 and 50 per cent of those responding accepted the need for wage and price regulation, at least as a reserve weapon against inflation.

More surprisingly, perhaps, the need for such intervention is implicit in the economic pronouncements of the Eisenhower Administration. The Administration has warned repeatedly that restraint is essential in wage and price making. The 1959 Economic Report of the President says, in remarkably categorial language, "Increases in money wages and other compensation not justified by the productivity performance of the economy are *inevitably* inflationary." It adds, "Self-discipline and restraint *are essential* if reasonable stability of prices is to be reached within the framework of free competitive institutions . . ." (Italics added.) Apart, perhaps, from its tendency to single out wages for special attention, the Administration accepts the argument of this chapter. Its only difference is in its belief that something will be accomplished by such warnings. This, of course, is pure nonsense. Professor Ben W. Lewis of Oberlin College has referred to these warnings as the policy of "creeping admonitionism" and he correctly points out that the policy has a long and perfect record of accomplishing nothing. One can scarcely imagine that the economists serving the President believe, themselves, that such warnings get results. Do they really wish to stake their professional reputations on the success of such a feeble course of policy?

In fact, these admonitions reflect only the tendency of our time which is for words to become not a portent of action but a substitute for it. But if one asks for effective action instead of words, the economic philosophy of the Eisenhower Administration brings one abruptly and inescapably to the issue of intervention in the setting of wages and prices.

Let me now suggest the principles that should govern such intervention.

8

First. Intervention should be limited. There is no need for public action where there is nothing wrong. Agricultural prices, those of the apparel industries and many others are set in highly unconcentrated markets of many sellers. Not being subject to control, these prices are not a cause of the inflation of which we are here speaking. So they need not be touched. In general where sellers are numerous, or labor is unorganized, or when prices have been stable or falling, there need be no intervention. Industries which by no stretch of the imagination could be considered important or pattern-setting should also be excluded. The value of the product is a not unserviceable test of importance. We should beware of the man who says, "If you control anything, you must control everything." To do everything will be to do nothing — which may be the aim of some who so warn.

Second. The machinery for intervention should be simple and its aim should be restraint, not rigid price- and wage-fixing. We are seeking to remove the inflationary effect of large increases in prices that are now at the discretion of steel, other metals, machinery, and other producers in the concentrated industries. And we are seeking to prevent wage increases in excess of what can be absorbed from requiring such advances or being the excuse for them. We can fall short of perfection in this effort and still improve vastly on the present discretionary price increases that are possible at full employment. The present situation, let us remind ourselves, allows, at full employment, for substantial price movements without restraint of any kind.

If we insist on absolute stability we shall also most likely end up doing nothing.

Third. The effort to achieve stability should, if at all possible, be carried on in a conciliatory spirit. Our problem is that in part of the economy prices are not stable at full employment. The task is to correct that defect, not to assess blame for its existence. Supervised self-regulation rather than control best describes what is required.

Almost any useful procedure will require an official finding each year of the wage advance that would be generally consistent with stable prices. (If the policy of admonition has no other fault, the total lack of any definition of what is reasonable and what is excessive is sufficient to render it worthless.) This finding should be arrived at only after full hearings and discussion. Then there should be tripartite committees in the relevant administered price industries which would represent labor, management, and the public in dealing in decentralized fashion with the application of the standards to that industry. If a new collective bargaining agreement required no price increase and none occurred, nothing further would be required.[3] Were it claimed that a wage advance would require higher prices, there would be investigation by the committee and finding of fact on its fairness and need. Certainly in the beginning, the sanctions of noncompliance should be mild and made with maximum reliance on the force of public opinion. However, we should remember that to concur in noncompliance is to discriminate against the man who cooperates. This machinery is not ideal, but it is better than unilateral control by the corporation or bipartite control by company and union.

We should also remind ourselves that the constant chase of wages by prices and prices by wages, which is our present situation is itself calculated to keep labor-management negotiations in a state of turmoil. The objective is to eliminate price inflation. To take this factor out of industrial relations would in turn greatly simplify and facilitate the very actions here suggested.

9

Professional guardians of our ideology will be prompt to say that proposals such as this infringe on the free price system. Therefore they are inconsistent, in principle, with the system of free markets. Second thoughts are in order. These

[3] Industries with large productivity gains would thus have an advantage, for they could advance wages without raising prices. And those with very small productivity gains would have to be allowed price advances to hold their labor. These anomalies must be accepted. It would be going to impractical extremes to require the industries with high productivity gains to reduce their prices. It is a sufficient advance to eliminate the large vertical changes which can and do occur and which have no relation to productivity changes.

proposals do not interfere with free markets. Rather they bring the public interest to bear on what is now, if one wishes to use harsh words, private price-fixing. If there is a case against the NRA type of price-setting authority, there is none against having the public interest represented where such authority already exists. It is obvious that if private discretion over prices did not exist, prices could not be raised in response to wage increases or for other reasons, and the problem with which we are here dealing would not arise. Where there is no such private price power, as in agriculture, the problem does not in fact arise.

Second, these proposals have a meaning for progressive government which goes considerably beyond the case for price stability. Inflation, because it is regressive, is unpopular. But it is not without conservative appeal. One must be a fairly imperturbable friend of the strong and the powerful to argue for it or to countenance it in its present form. But that means there are many who do not find it unpalatable.

And if some system of wage and price restraint is not available, the case for monetary and fiscal remedies for inflation will seem very strong. Monetary policy has a strong conservative appeal. It is well-liked by those with money to lend and by large corporate borrowers on whom the effect of a tight money policy is very slight. It has a restraining effect on public borrowing and spending by states and localities, which many consider fortunate.

Similarly fiscal policy can be a valuable talking point for the conservative. It now so serves. The price of more spending on education, health, defense, foreign aid, or conservation is, it is said, more inflation. Hence the man who opposes the expansion or improvement in these activities becomes the defender of the dollar. As one result, the bogy of inflation has now replaced the bogy of socialism as the barrier to enlarged and improved public services. And since inflation is a clear and present danger — a matter of recurring experience to many people — and socialism is not, it is a much more effective bogy.

This bogy would be exorcised if we had an effective way of dealing with inflation at full employment. Then the government could embark on needed and useful tasks when men and resources were unemployed. The imperatives of budget balancing would take over only when such resources were fully used. This, under a progressive economic policy, is when they should take over.

The liberal who wants full use of resources and steady growth and who opposes inflation does not have the additional luxury of deploring proposals such as those here advanced. Perhaps he can suggest improvements or more desirable alternatives. That is all the logic of the situation allows. There are imperatives of choice which a stern Providence does not allow even the most righteous man to avoid.

Part Two

How to Reread
History

V

The Moving Finger Sticks

THE MARK of a great historical event is that it changes
people or, more precisely, the way they think, so that
they are never quite the same again. And because they
hear so much about the event and then read about it, their
children and their children's children are also different. To
have this effect the event must be a matter of experience
to all or a large majority of a people. And that experience
must be one of deep sorrow, fear, or pain. As people are
constituted it is the extreme and perhaps also the seemingly
unjustified suffering which has profound effect. It is truly
said that people never know when they are well off.

The point is readily verified. In Britain the vast bloodbath
of World War I still gives to the word *war* its special con-
notation. The reason is that nothing in Britain since —
certainly nothing in World War II — carried such a connota-
tion of horror for so many as the boarding of the train for
France and the front in the reasonable certainty of an almost uniquely dismal death. This was a war, we should recall, in which no man posted to active service on the Western
Front could reasonably expect to survive. The average combat life of a British first lieutenant was between two days
and two weeks.

The experience of the United States in the First World War was very different, and so also was the experience in World War II. In each case, the number directly involved in combat was very small in relation to the total population. Only a minority, accordingly, had to contemplate their own certain slaughter. On the contrary, and especially in World War II, a large number of people found pleasure in jobs they had never expected to have, in responsibility which they had never expected to assume, in travel previously reserved to the rich, and in escape from worthy but routine wives. As a result these wars were not for us events of profound historical consequence. It may be guessed that if a majority of Americans had experienced life in Heutgen forest or had been present on the edge of Hiroshima, the subsequent talk of movements to the brink would have been regarded with much less equanimity.

Although the two world wars fail the test, it is easy to select the two events of the last century which did have a deep historical impact. The first was the Civil War. The second was the Great Depression.

2

A case can be made that of the two the Great Depression had the greater impact. In the Confederacy the trauma of war and its aftermath was profound. The tedium and discomforts of military service and the perils of combat were widely experienced. Armies passed and fought and the war ended with military occupation and surrender of sovereignty. Everyone suffered from the inflation and economic disarray and many from hunger and privation. Finally, there was a partial revolution in social structure and the threat of a far greater one. Not only did few escape these consequences but few were meant to escape. "We are not only fighting hostile armies, but a hostile people," said Sherman, "and must make old and young, rich and poor, feel the hand of war, as well as their organized armies." [1] Thaddeus Stevens and his friends were equally determined.

But this was a regional tragedy. Save for the departure, danger, and death of those who were in the armies, the North had none of these sorrows. Prices rose, but rising prices were a highly mitigated misfortune. They made farmers happy and business good. Everywhere industry and commerce were expanding. Gettysburg was the only important battlefield above the Border. It is not surprising that the South remembered the war as the North did not.

The Great Depression, in contrast, left no part of the nation and very few individuals untouched. Workingmen became unemployed or lived in fear that they would. There was no unemployment compensation on which they could expect to land. Farmers went bankrupt or feared they would. Nor was there anyone to whom they could hope to turn. Economic misfortune had a hopeless terminal quality in those days. And even in the depression the unemployed worker and the broken farmer could not entirely escape the ethos, some of it the residue of social Darwinism, that unemployment or bankruptcy marked a man as an inferior being. The middle class and the rich had their sorrows too. Their fortunes fell with the stock market and Associated Gas

[1] *Memoirs*, Vol. II, p. 27. Quoted by Clement Eaton, *A History of the Southern Confederacy*. New York: Macmillan, 1934.

& Electric. American industry supports a sizable privileged caste in jobs of considerable prestige and some pecuniary reward. In the depression this leisured aristocracy was combed out. And, as in the Confederacy, there was the fear, if not the reality, of social revolution. Lincoln's intentions were regarded as little more malignant in South Carolina than Mr. Roosevelt's on Long Island. It is significant that the historical appetite which sustains the vast outpouring of work on Lincoln, the generals, and their campaigns is equaled only by the literature of Roosevelt, his lieutenants, and the New Deal.

Events that are as deeply remembered as the Civil War and the Great Depression are remembered because they have burned themselves into the minds and consciousness of people. In so changing people they change the course of history, and that is why they are important. This in turn creates grave dangers to historical understanding. For precisely because these events have created such a profound popular impression, they will have from the beginning a popular explanation. The interpretation that first gains acceptance will normally reflect an incomplete, emotional, or perhaps an obsolescent view. This interpretation will then take leave of the realm of science and even of history and enter that of folklore. It will not be easily susceptible to reinterpretation in the light either of later ideas or later evidence. We are less likely to have an understanding of great events than of lesser ones because we are far more massively committed to the wrong view. This problem of stereotypes is readily illustrated from the history of the Civil War and the Great Depression. It will be convenient, reversing the usual sequence of history, to look first at some of the common views of the Great Depression.

3

The history of the Roosevelt recovery program is dominated by three or four great measures — the NRA, the Agricultural Adjustment Act, the gold-buying program, and the relief and public works programs. Of these the centerpiece was the NRA. It was so regarded then, and it still dominates the New Deal histories. The stereotype is firm. It was one of Roosevelt's heroic mistakes. In seeking by direct action to arrest deflation — to put a floor under wages and prices — he was seeking to do the impossible in the wrong way. Not unaccountably the task was bungled and, when the Supreme Court in the Schechter Case finally declared the National Industrial Recovery Act unconstitutional, it rescued Roosevelt from grave error and the country from the even graver danger of a colossal cartelization quite at odds with its traditions of free competition.

This view of NRA will never be much altered.[2] Yet an economic historian now examining the matter afresh could readily reach very different conclusions. In the modern industrial market under conditions of severe deflation, price cutting could force wage cutting and the latter, in turn, permits of more price cutting in an evil downward spiral. That was the condition with which NRA sought to contend. And when demand is strong it is equally evident that wage increases can be both a cause and an excuse for price increases

[2] Though a different one is offered by Arthur M. Schlesinger, Jr., in *The Coming of the New Deal*. Boston: Houghton Mifflin, 1959, pp. 172 et seq.

and these can lead on to further increases in wages. The spiral then winds upward. This is the problem for which we now seek a remedy. As the last chapter has shown, there must be some arrangement between corporations, unions, and government if we are to reconcile high employment with price stability.

The NRA was wretchedly administered and its designers and managers probably saw rather poorly what it was supposed to do. But it may well have reflected a more realistic view of market processes than was held by those who, accepting the doctrine of the market, argued that in the absence of such intervention all would necessarily work out admirably. But the first judgment on NRA was given by those who were committed to a sanguine view — who held to the traditional model of the competitive society. Since they had not accepted the passing of the latter society, they unreservedly welcomed the passing of NRA. Their view has now become part of the folk wisdom of the country. It will not be reversed.

As just noted, NRA ranks with the Agricultural Adjustment Administration, devaluation, and the relief and public works programs as one of the pedestals of early New Deal policy. It was launched with a mighty fanfare — there was the Blue Eagle, the longest parade in history, and the inspired expletives of General Hugh S. Johnson who was indeed one of the great masters of polemical English. All this impressed the historians as it did the people — and still does. Yet with the assistance of later knowledge another measure might well be accorded equal attention.

In 1933, as part of the Glass-Steagall Banking Act of that

year, the Congress provided for the insurance of bank de-
posits. This changed a highly decentralized banking system
into a relatively interdependent one. It marked — that is to
say it truly marked — the end of an era. Never again would
the long lines form outside the banks in response to the
rumor that something was wrong inside. Never again would
the failure of one bank bring down another and that one
yet others in a tenpin effect. Never again would there be
the grief and panic so grimly associated with bank failure.
It is hard to imagine a reform more important than this.
It had no Hugh Johnson, no Robbie, no parade. A few
beaten conservatives said it was socialist, and subsided.
Consequently, it rates only a line or two in the history books.
Yet, compared with deposit insurance, NRA was a passing
show.

4

Now we may go a step further back to the second of the
great events — the Civil War. Here the stereotypes are even
more in need of re-examination. The two world wars taught
us much about the problems of war mobilization. However
these lessons have never been applied retrospectively to the
assessment of the Civil War management. Equally important, Keynes has released economics from doctrines which
insured that almost any interpretation of Civil War finance
would be gravely misleading. But the history has not been
emancipated. The result is that the Civil War experience,
especially its economic and administrative history, is profoundly obscured by the contemporary myth.

Thus nothing is more nearly agreed than that the civil

management of the Civil War was exceedingly bad. Procurement was indifferently handled. Fraud, profiteering and speculation were rife. Sacrifice was unequally shared or not shared at all. This mismanagement loomed large in the contemporary view. "The passion for speculation," President Davis said in 1863, "has seduced citizens of all classes from a determined prosecution of the war to a sordid effort to amass money." Lincoln was equally plain. And so was the common soldier who spoke freely of the "rich man's war and the poor man's fight." Exceptions to this dismal story are recognized — the work of Josiah Gorgas in procuring arms for the Confederate armies and that of McCallum and Haupt in organizing railroad transport for the Union — but the impression remains one of exceptional incompetence.

Nothing has been more severely assailed than the management of Civil War finance. The Union did not tax soon enough. The Confederacy scarcely taxed at all. Both sides showed a soft-headed belief that they could get by with borrowing and the issue of paper money. To speak of an "issue of greenbacks" is still to imply loose and evil financial policy. But Southern practice was infinitely worse. Channing noted that: "Northern writers of an economic turn of mind have oftentimes attributed the collapse of the Confederacy to its paper money, over-issues of bonds, and the impressment." [3]

The management of the Civil War was certainly no model of austerity, rigor and perfection. Many things — the buying of substitutes and the exemption of the larger slave-

[3] *History of the United States* (New York: Macmillan, 1925), Vol. VI, p. 411.

holders — fare worse, not better, when later standards are applied. Yet both governments accommodated themselves with remarkable speed and vigor to the urgencies of the moment and to the resources, both physical and administrative, which they had at hand. Armies of great size were speedily equipped and got into the field. It has long been a matter of comment that the Union armies were provided with a remarkable variety of weapons of remarkably heterogeneous performance. But the price of standardization would have been delay in equipping the force. This would have been more serious. That there was waste in procurement, that profits were high, and that there was fraud is beyond question. Simon Cameron, the nineteenth century Grundy who was Lincoln's first Secretary of War, was a painful mistake. But would more careful and meticulous review of contracts, more careful policing for fraud, more centralization in Washington have served the Union cause? Again the price would have been time, of which there was none. In the case of the Union armies we do well to remember that one of the complaints has been that they were too luxuriously supplied.[4] Meigs, the Quartermaster General of the Union, clearly sensed the urgencies of his task and acted accordingly. The Confederates, he knew, would not wait till things were properly organized. So, ignoring his critics, he got the supplies. His critics have had the best of it ever since.

However, it is on financial administration that another

[4] "No army before had been so lavishly supplied with food, clothing, and equipment as were Union soldiers after 1861. They were weighted down with impedimenta which they threw away at the first moments of fatigue, to the delight of the Confederates." Channing, pp. 406–7.

view is most needed. The history of the Civil War has been written almost exclusively by friends of hard money.[5] They did not consider the alternatives open to the warring governments. Nor, on the whole, did they consider results. They condemned the policies that were followed, successful or otherwise, as a matter of principle.

Viewed in a modern light, a moderate amount of inflation was unquestionably least of evils for the North. It would not have been sensible to delay mobilization until tax revenues were yielding the requisite return. We are now far less impressed by the difference between noninterest-bearing securities (the greenbacks) and interest-bearing loans as causes of inflation. Under conditions of full employment both would now be regarded as inflationary. And in the wartime North rising prices gave an impetus to the economy. They helped to offset the dislocation caused by the loss of Southern market and Southern cotton supplies. Confederate doctrine, in one of those hopeful miscalculations which seem so much a part of our history, had counted heavily on these effects to bring the commercially minded Northerners to terms. "No! You dare not make war upon cotton; no power on earth dares make war upon it . . . who can doubt, that has looked on recent events, that cotton is supreme?" [6]

[5] I should here exclude the most complete and scholarly study of Civil War finance, that of Wesley Clair Mitchell of Northern finance. (A History of the Greenbacks. Chicago: University of Chicago Press, 1903.) Mitchell disapproved of the greenbacks but not on doctrinaire grounds. However, a number of his adverse conclusions would now be open to challenge. Also, his was not a contemporary study. By 1903, nearly forty years after the end of the war, attitudes on wartime financial policy had hardened.

[6] Governor James H. Hammond of South Carolina, March 4, 1858. Quoted by Frederick Law Olmstead, The Cotton Kingdom (New York: Knopf, 1953), p. 7.

From 1860 to 1865, according to the patient researches of Wesley C. Mitchell, retail prices a little less than doubled and wholesale prices a little more than doubled.[7] Was this so bad for a nation torn in two, unaided by modern controls, fighting for its existence in the greatest war in history? On the contrary, it was phenomenally good.

A less good case can be made for Confederate financial practice. In the South the aversion to taxes was extreme — by common estimate only about one per cent of the war-time expenditure was raised in this way. Yet, once again, it is hardly reasonable to suggest that the armies should have been held back until Congress in Richmond had been persuaded to levy taxes and the states and people to pay them. A nation that defended its independence on the theory of state sovereignty was bound to have difficulties in this regard. And it is impossible to suppress a certain admiration for the sheer audacity of Confederate financial legerdemain. A raw agricultural country sustained a vast army — the size is perhaps the most disputed statistic of our history, but evidently between 600,000 and a million men were enlisted and after a fashion equipped — for four years of heavy combat and under conditions of partial occupation and blockade. All this it accomplished on *total* cash resources of gold or its hard money equivalent of some $27,000,000. It would be interesting to see how the Pentagon would go about fighting this war on this sum.

5

However the greatest stereotype of the Civil War concerns the consequences attributed to it in the South. When peace

[7] *Op cit.*, p. 264. These are unweighted averages.

came, the ruined cities of the South were quickly restored. A mere fifteen years after the end of the war, cotton production was above ante bellum levels. This, no doubt, was a fair index of recovery elsewhere in the economy. Yet the conviction remains to this day that the war put a permanent blight on the fortunes of the entire region.

This is most often traced to the complete though mystical destruction of the capital of the South. Much of this went with the slaves. What the Beards called "the most stupendous act of sequestration in the history of Anglo-Saxon jurisprudence," [8] eliminated at one stroke perhaps four billion dollars worth of wealth. Meanwhile, savings which had gone into the bonds and currency of the Confederacy became worthless, and physical property was destroyed. These were staggering blows from which, serious men still say, the South never recovered.

None of this makes sense by any modern view. The capital in the slaves was not destroyed. It was transferred from plantation owner to freedman, and there was social loss only so far as the labor produced by the latter was less efficient. It may have been less efficient, but the full recovery of cotton production within two decades following the war shows that the management of the free labor was no insuperable problem.

During the war years the savings of the South were used to buy arms and ammunition as was so in the North. The Confederate bonds that became worthless were the claims of those who had supplied savings to repayment with inter-

8 *The Rise of American Civilization* (New York: Macmillan, revised 1-volume ed., 1934), p. 100.

est out of later public revenues. They weren't repaid, which meant that the revenue remained with other persons for other use. It might have been more of a drag on recovery to have levied the necessary taxes to service and redeem the Confederate debt.

The physical capital of the South suffered, but the impression of enduring harm must be squared with the rapid rebuilding. Moreover, all the references to the destruction of the capital of the South implies that these states were a separate capital market with a supply of capital that was peculiarly their own. This is nonsense. After the war the Confederacy was again part of the Union. We should expect capital, like the carpetbaggers, to pursue profit to the South as it did to the West. Perhaps the opportunity was not there. In the economist's terms there would seem to be a strong probability that the marginal efficiency of capital in the South in the decades following Reconstruction was relatively low.

There is another thing on which we might reflect. Following World War I and especially following World War II, the belligerent countries made a rapid recovery. At least by superficial comparison the wartime and post–World War II misfortunes of West Germany could hardly have been less than those of the Confederacy. It suffered frightful capital destruction, had a currency that became virtually valueless, bonds that were all but repudiated, and it was occupied rather more elaborately than the Confederacy. Yet in less than a decade German living standards had fully recovered; industrial production was at record levels; so was capital formation; and foreign trade had never been so flourishing.

Why should a war blight the South for a century and usher in Germany's most prosperous years?

It would seem possible that the South was in a bad way before the war — that it had, in fact, an obsolescent agrarian economy in which poverty was disguised by slavery and the power, prestige and income of a considerable ruling class on which all attention centered. After the war, in an age of rapidly advancing industrialization, such a purely agricultural area was bound to seem even more backward. And now the prewar poverty was less visibly relieved by a well-to-do planter class while the freedman had to be counted in.

We may go on to speculate as to why industry came later to this part of the country. Perhaps it was a late start, in which slavery played a part. Perhaps it was an accident of commerce routes and geography and the course of immigration. There are many other possible reasons, and among them the war would seem to be among the least.

It has often been said that every generation rewrites history to its own tastes and specifications. This would appear to be unduly optimistic. Where great events are concerned there is every evidence that the moving finger sticks.

VI

The Care and Prevention of Disaster

THE DECADE of the twenties, or more precisely the eight
years between the postwar depression of 1920–21 and
the stock market crash in October of 1929, were prosperous
ones in the United States. The total output of the economy
increased by more than 50 per cent. The preceding decades
had brought the automobile; now came many more automobiles and also roads on which they could be driven with
reasonable reliability and comfort. The downtown section
of the mid-continent city — Des Moines, Omaha, Minne-
apolis — dates to these years. It was then, more likely than
not, that what is still the leading hotel, the tallest office
building, and the biggest department store went up.

These years were also remarkable in another respect, for
as time passed, it became increasingly evident that the prosperity could not last. Contained within it were the seeds
of its own destruction. Herein lies the peculiar fascination
of the period for a study in the problem of leadership. For
almost no steps were taken during these years to arrest tendencies which were obviously leading, and which did lead,
to disaster.

❋

2

At least four things were seriously wrong, and they worsened as the decade passed. And knowledge of them does not depend on the always brilliant assistance of hindsight. At least three of these flaws were highly visible and widely discussed. In ascending order, not of importance but of visibility, they were as follows:

First, income in these prosperous years was being distributed with marked inequality. Although output per worker rose steadily during the period, wages were fairly stable as also were prices. As a result, business profits increased rapidly and so did incomes of the wealthy and the well-to-do. This tendency was nurtured by the assiduous and successful efforts of Secretary of the Treasury Andrew W. Mellon to reduce income taxes with special attention to the higher brackets. In 1929 the 5 per cent of the people with the highest incomes received perhaps a third of all personal income, and those at the very top were increasing their share.[1] This meant that the economy was heavily and increasingly dependent on the luxury consumption of the well-to-do and on their willingness to reinvest what they did not or could not spend on themselves. Anything that shocked the confidence of the rich either in their personal or in their business future would have a bad effect on total spending and hence on the behavior of the economy.

This was the least visible flaw. To be sure farmers, who were not participating in the general advance, were making

[1] Cf. my *The Great Crash, 1929* (Boston: Houghton Mifflin, 1955), pp. 179–183.

themselves heard; and twice during the period the Congress passed far-reaching farm relief legislation which was vetoed by Coolidge. But other groups were much less vocal. Income distribution in the United States had long been unequal. The inequality of these years did not seem exceptional. The trade union movement was also far from strong, and labor was little heard from. In the early twenties the steel industry was still working a twelve-hour day and a seven-day week. (Every two weeks, when the shift changed, a man worked twice around the clock.) Workers lacked the organization or the organizing power to deal even with conditions like this, and the twelve-hour day was, in fact, ended as the result of personal pressure by President Harding on the steel companies.[2] In all these circumstances the increasingly lopsided income did not excite much comment or alarm. Perhaps it would have been surprising if it had.

But the other three flaws in the economy were far less subtle. During World War I the United States ceased to be the world's greatest debtor country and became its greatest creditor. The consequences of this change have been so often described that they have the standing of a cliché. A debtor country could export a greater value of goods than it imported and use the difference for interest and debt repayment. This was what we did before the First World War. But a creditor must import a greater value than it exports if those who owe it money are to have the where-

[2] In particular on Judge Elbert H. Gary, the lawyer who was head of the United States Steel Corporation. Judge Gary's personal acquaintance with these working conditions was thought to be slight, and this gave rise to Benjamin Stolberg's classic sally that the Judge "never saw a blast furnace until his death."

withal to pay interest and principal. Otherwise the creditor must either forgive the debts or make new loans to pay off the old.[3]

During the twenties the balance was maintained by making new foreign loans. Their promotion was profitable to domestic investment houses. And when the supply of honest and competent foreign borrowers ran out, dishonest, incompetent or fanciful borrowers were invited to borrow and, on occasion, bribed to do so. In 1927 Juan Leguia, the son of the current dictator of Peru, was paid $450,000 by the National City Company, an affiliate of the National City Bank, and by J. & W. Seligman for his services in promoting a $50,000,000 loan to Peru which these houses marketed. Americans lost and the Peruvians didn't gain much. Other Latin American republics got equally dubious loans by equally dubious devices. And for reasons that now tax the imagination, so did a large number of German cities and municipalities. Obviously, once investors awoke to the character of these loans, or there was any other shock to confidence, they would no longer be made. There would be nothing with which to pay the old loans. Given this arithmetic, there would be either a sharp reduction in exports, or a wholesale default on the outstanding loans, or more likely both. Wheat and cotton farmers and others who depended on exports would suffer. So would those who owned the bonds. The buying power of both would be reduced. These consequences were freely predicted at the time.

---

[3] In modern times two new correctives of imbalance have come into extensive use. These are government loans and gifts. In the twenties government loans were not yet a peacetime commonplace, and large-scale public gifts as yet uninvented, at least by the United States.

The second weakness of the economy was the large-scale corporate thimble-rigging that was going on. This took a variety of forms of which by far the most common was the organization of corporations to hold stock in yet other corporations which, in turn, held stock in yet other corporations. In the case of the railroad and the utilities, the purpose of this pyramid of holding companies was to obtain control of a very large number of operating companies with a very small investment in the ultimate holding company. A hundred million dollar electric utility, of which the capitalization was represented half by bonds and half by common stock, could be controlled with an investment of a little over twenty-five million — the value of just over half the common stock. Were a company then formed with the same capital structure to hold *this* twenty-five million worth of common stock, it could be controlled with an investment of $6.25 million. On the next round the amount required would be less than two million. That two million would still control the entire hundred million dollar edifice. By the end of the twenties holding company structures six or eight tiers high were commonplace. Some of them — the utility pyramid of Insull and Associated Gas & Electric, and the railroad pyramid of the Van Sweringens — were marvelously complex. It is unlikely that anyone fully understood them or could.

In other cases companies were organized to hold securities in other companies and thus to manufacture more securities to sell to the public. This was true of the great investment trusts. During 1929 one investment house, Goldman, Sachs & Company, organized and sold nearly a billion dollars worth of securities in three interconnected investment trusts — Goldman, Sachs Trading Corporation, Shenandoah Corporation, and the Blue Ridge Corporation. All eventually depreciated virtually to nothing. This was, perhaps, the greatest financial fiasco in our history.

This corporate insanity was also highly visible. So was the damage. The pyramids would last only so long as earnings of the company at the bottom were secure. If anything happened to the dividends of the underlying company, there would be trouble for upstream companies that had issued bonds (or in practice sometimes preferred stock) against the dividends on the stock of the downstream companies. Once the earnings stopped, the bonds would go into default or the preferred stock would take over and the pyramid would collapse. Such a collapse would have a bad effect not only on the orderly prosecution of business and investment by the operating companies but also on confidence, investment, and spending by the community at large. The likelihood was increased because in a number of cities — Cleveland, Detroit, and Chicago were notable examples — the banks were deeply committed to these pyramids or had fallen under the control of the pyramiders.

Finally, and most evident of all, was the stock market boom. Month after month and year after year, prices rose and people became increasingly preoccupied with the market. In May of 1924 the *New York Times* industrials stood at 106; by the end of the year they were 134; by the end of 1925 they were up to 181. In 1927 the advance began in earnest — to 245 by the end of that year and on to 331 by the end of 1928. There were some setbacks in early

1929, but then came the fantastic summer explosion when in a matter of three months the averages went up another 110 points. This was perhaps the most frantic summer in our financial history. By its end stock prices had quadrupled as compared with four years earlier. Transactions on the New York Stock Exchange regularly ran to five million or more shares a day. Radio (adjusted) went to 505 without ever having paid a dividend. Only the old-fashioned or the eccentric held securities for their income. What counted was the increase in capital values.

And since capital gains were what counted, one could vastly increase his opportunities by extending his holdings with borrowed funds — by buying on margin. Margin accounts expanded enormously, and from all over the country, indeed from all over the world, money poured into New York to finance these transactions. During the summer of 1929 brokers' loans increased at the rate of $400,000,000 a month. By September they totaled more than $7,000,000,-000. The rate of interest on these loans varied from 7 to 12 per cent and went as high as 15.

The boom was also inherently self-liquidating. It could last only as long as new people, or at least new money, was pouring into the market in pursuit of the capital gains. This new demand bid up the stocks and made the capital gains. Once the supply of new customers began to falter, the market would cease to rise. Once the market stopped rising there would be no more gains and some, perhaps a good many, would start to cash in. If you are concerned with capital gains, you must get them while the getting is good. But the getting will start the market down, and this would one day be the signal for much more selling — both by those who were trying to get out and those who were being forced to sell securities that were no longer safely margined. Thus the market was certain one day to go down and far more rapidly than it went up. Down it went with a thunderous crash in October of 1929. In a series of terrible days, of which Thursday, October 24, and Tuesday, October 29, were the most terrifying, billions in values were lost, and thousands of speculators — they had been called investors — were utterly and totally ruined.

This too had far-reaching effects. Economists have rather deprecated the tendency to attribute too much to the great stock market collapse of 1929. That was the drama. The causes of the subsequent depression really lay deeper. In fact, the stock market crash was very important. It exposed the other weakness of the economy. The overseas loans on which the payments balance depended came to an end. The jerry-built holding company structures came tumbling down. The investment trust stocks collapsed. The crash put a marked crimp on borrowing for investment and therewith on business spending. It also removed from the economy some billions of consumer spending that was either based on, sanctioned by, or encouraged by stock market gains. The crash was an intensely damaging thing.

And this damage, too, was not only foreseeable but fore-seen. For months the speculative frenzy had all but dominated American life. Many times before in history — the South Sea Bubble, John Law's speculations, the recurrent real estate booms of the Nineteenth Century, the Florida land boom earlier in the same decade — there had been similar frenzy. And the end had always come not with a whimper but a bang. Many men, including in 1929 the President of the United States, knew it would again be so.

3

The increasingly perilous trade balance, the corporate buccaneering and the Wall Street boom — along with less visible tendencies in income distribution — were all allowed to proceed to the ultimate disaster without hindrance. What blame attaches to the men who were charged with national leadership?

Warren G. Harding died on August 3, 1923. This, as only death can, exonerates him. Few of the disorders which led eventually to such trouble were well started when the fatal blood clot formed in the veins of this now sad and deeply disillusioned man. Some would argue that his legacy was bad. Harding had but a vague perception of the economic processes over which he presided. He died owing his broker $180,000 in a blind account — he had been speculating disastrously while he was President. No one so inclined would have been a good bet to curb the coming boom. Two of Harding's cabinet officers, his Secretary of the Interior and his Attorney General, were to plead the Fifth Amendment when faced with questions concerning their official acts, and the first of these went to jail. Harding brought his fellow townsman, Daniel R. Crissinger, to be his Comptroller of the Currency, although he was qualified for this task, as one historian has suggested, only by the fact that he and the young Harding had stolen watermelons together.[4] When Crissinger had had an ample opportunity to demonstrate

[4] Samuel Hopkins Adams, *The Incredible Era.* Boston: Houghton Mifflin, 1939.

his incompetence in his first post, he was made head of the Federal Reserve System. He had the central responsibility for action in the ensuing boom. Jack Dempsey, Paul Whiteman, or F. Scott Fitzgerald would have been equally qualified.

Yet the fact remains that Harding was dead before the real trouble started. And while he left in office some very poor men, he also left some very competent ones. Charles Evans Hughes, his Secretary of State; Herbert Hoover, his Secretary of Commerce; and Henry C. Wallace, his Secretary of Agriculture, were public servants of vigor and judgment. They were more than the equal of their counterparts on Eisenhower's team.

4

The problem of Herbert Hoover's responsibility is more complicated. He became President on March 4, 1929. At first glance this seems far too late for effective action. By then the damage had been done, and while the crash might come a little sooner or a little later, it was now (as Mr. Hoover has said) inevitable. Yet Hoover's involvement was deeper than this, and certainly much deeper than Harding's. This he tacitly concedes in his memoirs, for he is at great pains to explain and even excuse himself.

For one thing, Hoover was no newcomer to Washington. He had been Secretary of Commerce under Harding and Coolidge. He had also been the strongest figure (not entirely excluding the President) in the Executive for approaching eight years. He had a clear view of what was going on. As early as 1922, in a letter to Hughes, he expressed grave concern over the quality of the foreign loans that were being floated in New York. He returned several times to the subject. He knew about the corporate thimble-rigging. In the later twenties he wrote to his colleagues and fellow officials (including Crissinger) expressing his grave concern over the Wall Street orgy. Yet he was content to express himself — to write letters and memoranda, or at most, as in the case of the foreign loans, to make an occasional speech. He could with complete propriety have taken his views of the stock market to the Congress. He could also have maintained a vigorous and persistent agitation within the Administration. And he could have sought to persuade the public of the dangers he saw. He did none of these things. His views of the market were so deeply concealed that it celebrated his election and inauguration with a great upsurge. Hoover was in the boat and, as he himself tells, he knew where it was headed. But having quietly warned the man at the tiller, he rode along into the reef.

And even though trouble was inevitable by March 1929, a truly determined man would still have wanted to do something. Nothing else was so important. The resources of the Executive, one might expect, would have been mobilized in a search for some formula to mitigate the current frenzy and to temper the coming crash. The assistance of the bankers, congressional leaders, and the Exchange authorities would have been sought. Nothing of the sort was done. Previously, as he later explained, he had thought himself frustrated by Mellon. But he continued Mellon in office. Henry M. Robinson, a sympathetic Los Angeles banker, was commissioned to go to New York to see his colleagues there and report. He returned to say that the New York bankers regarded things as sound. Richard Whitney, the vice-president of the Stock Exchange, was summoned to the White House for a conference on how to curb speculation. Nothing came of this either. Whitney also thought things were sound.

Both Mr. Hoover and his official biographers carefully explain that the primary responsibility for the goings on in New York City rested not with Washington but with the Governor of New York State. That was Franklin D. Roosevelt. It was he who failed to rise to his responsibilities. The explanation is unpersuasive. The future of the whole country was involved. Mr. Hoover was the President of the whole country. If he lacked authority commensurate with this responsibility, he could have requested it. This, Roosevelt, at a later date, did not hesitate to do.

Finally, while by March of 1929 the stock market collapse was inevitable, something could still have been done about the other accumulating disorders. The balance of payments is an obvious case. In 1931, Mr. Hoover did request a one year's moratorium on the interallied (war) debts. This was a courageous and constructive step which came directly to grips with the problem. But the year before, Mr. Hoover, though not without reluctance, had signed the Smoot-Hawley tariff, while shifting responsibility to his party. "I shall approve the Tariff Bill . . . It was undertaken as the result of pledges given by the Republican Party at Kansas City . . . Platform promises must not be empty gestures." [5] No step could have been more directly designed to make things

[5] Memorandum analyzing the legislation. From *The Memoirs of Herbert Hoover* (New York: Macmillan, 1952), Vol. 1, p. 297.

worse. Countries would have even more trouble earning the dollars of which they were so desperately short. This was pointed out by hundreds of people, from Albert H. Wiggin, the heavily involved head of the Chase National Bank, to Oswald Garrison Villard, the editor of the *Nation*. But Mr. Hoover went ahead and signed the bill.

5

Anyone familiar with this particular race of men knows that a dour, flinty, inscrutable visage such as that of Calvin Coolidge can be the mask for a calm and acutely perceptive intellect. And he knows equally that it can conceal a mind of singular aridity. The difficulty, given the inscrutability, is in knowing which. However, in the case of Coolidge, the evidence is in favor of the second. In some sense, he probably knew what was going on. A Coolidge could scarcely have been unaware of what was called the Coolidge market. But he connected developments neither with the well-being of the country nor with his own responsibilities. In his memoirs Hoover goes to great lengths to show how closely he was in touch with events and how clearly he foresaw their consequences. In his *Autobiography,* a notably barren document, Coolidge does not refer at all to the accumulating troubles. He is concerned only with such unequivocal truths as "The President stands at the head of all official and social rank in the nation"; "Every day of Presidential life is crowded with activities" (which in his case was not true); and "The Congress makes the laws, but it is the President who causes them to be executed." [6]

[6] *The Autobiography of Calvin Coolidge.* New York: The Cosmopolitan Book Corporation, 1929.

At various times during his years in office men called on Coolidge to warn him of the impending trouble. And in 1927 at the instigation of a former White House aide he sent for William Z. Ripley of Harvard, the most articulate critic of the corporate machinations of the period. The President listened carefully while Ripley described (as Ripley later told) the "prestidigitation, double-shuffling, honeyfugling, hornswoggling, and skulduggery" that characterized the current Wall Street scene. Coolidge asked Ripley to stay for lunch and to go into more detail. But Ripley made the mistake of telling Coolidge that regulation was the responsibility of the states. At this intelligence Coolidge's face lit up and he dismissed the entire matter from mind. Others got even less far.

And on some occasions Coolidge added fuel to the fire. If the market seemed to be faltering, a timely statement from the White House — or possibly from Secretary Mellon — would often brace it up. William Allen White, by no means an unfriendly observer, noted that after one such comment the market staged a 26-point rise. He went on to say, though perhaps with some exaggeration, that a careful search "during these halcyon years . . . discloses this fact: Whenever the stock market showed signs of weakness, the President or the Secretary of the Treasury or some important dignitary of the administration . . . issued a statement. The statement invariably declared that business was 'fundamentally sound,' that continued prosperity had arrived, and that the slump of the moment was 'seasonal.' " [7]

[7] *A Puritan in Babylon* (New York: The Macmillan Company, 1939), p. 334. White also tells of the Ripley visit.

Such was the Coolidge role. Coolidge was fond of observing that "if you see ten troubles coming down the road, you can be sure that nine will run into the ditch before they reach you and you have to battle with only one of them." One of his critics noted that "the trouble with this philosophy was that when the tenth trouble reached him he was wholly unprepared . . . The outstanding instance was the rising boom and orgy of mad speculation which began in 1927." The critic was Herbert Hoover.[8]

6

Plainly the leadership in these years failed. Events, the tragic culmination of which could be foreseen and which was foreseen, were allowed to work themselves out to the final disaster. The country and the world paid. For a time, indeed, the very reputation of capitalism itself was in the balance. It survived in the years ahead perhaps less because of its own power or esteem than because of the absence of an organized and plausible alternative. Yet one important question remains. Would it have been possible even for a strong leadership to arrest the plunge? Were not the opposing forces too strong? Isn't one asking the impossible?

The answer depends less on the man who was President than on the social and political context in which whoever is President finds himself. That of Coolidge and Hoover, though it was partly of their own creation, probably made decisive leadership impossible. These were conservative administrations in which, in addition, the influence of the busi-

[8] *Memoirs,* Vol. I, pp. 55–56.

nessman was strong. Concerning one characteristic of the great business executive in public office, one can generalize with nearly perfect confidence: he is reluctant to react to unrealized dangers. If something hasn't happened, it may not happen. As a result, one should wait and see if things will work out. Let there be no hasty action.

This instinct is deeply grounded. At the core of the conservative faith there was still in 1929, and there lurks today, an intuitive belief in laissez-faire — in the benign tendency of things that are left alone. The man who wants to intervene, by contrast, must be regarded with suspicion. He is a meddler. Perhaps, indeed, he is a planner. There is, in fact, no more important public function than the suppression of proposals for unneeded action. But these *must* be distinguished from needed action. The characteristic business leader in high position tends to oppose both.

The most reviled figure of the Harding-Coolidge-Hoover era, not excepting Secretary Albert B. Fall of Teapot Dome, was Treasury Secretary Andrew W. Mellon. He opposed all action to curb the boom, although once in 1929 he was persuaded to say that bonds (as distinct from stocks) were a good buy. And when the depression came, he was against doing anything about that. Mr. Hoover was shocked by his insistence that the only remedy for economic distress was (as Mr. Hoover characterized it) to "liquidate labor, liquidate stocks, liquidate the farmers, liquidate real estate." Yet Mellon reflected only in extreme form the conviction that things would work out, that the real enemies were those who interfered. His position was not essentially different or even more unreasonable than that of the business leaders who resisted a cutback in car production to make way for arms in the early years of World War II or those who, in more recent times, shared the honest conviction of George M. Humphrey and Charles E. Wilson that the major threat to our national safety came from the advocates of new and expensive Federal programs and that the real threat to our national existence came from those who would spend us into some unspecified form of national bankruptcy. Obviously a President who has surrounded himself with such men has given strong hostages to inaction. The great executive, in the popular cliché, is a symbol of action. In making and selling things he may be. But in Washington, subject always to exceptions, he is not.

Moreover, government is not a thing apart. Those who lead it are not automatons divorced from the world outside. They still have friends. They are still subject, in greater or less measure, to the dictates or the pressure of the group or community to which they belong. Outside of Washington in the twenties the business and banking community, or at least the articulate part of it, was overwhelmingly opposed to any public intervention. The tentative and wholly ineffective steps which the Federal Reserve did take to check the boom were strongly criticized. In the spring of 1929, when the Reserve System seemed to be on the verge of taking more decisive action, there was an anticipatory tightening of money rates for buying securities and a sharp drop in the market. On his own initiative Charles E. Mitchell, the head of the National City Bank, poured new funds into the market. He had an obligation, he said, that was "paramount to any Federal Reserve warning, or anything else" to avert a crisis in the money market. Mitchell was a director of the New York Federal Reserve Bank. In that same spring, Paul M. Warburg, a distinguished and respected Wall Street leader, warned of the dangers of the boom and called for action to restrain it. He was deluged with criticism, even abuse, and later confessed that the subsequent days were the most difficult of his life. Others avoided similar pressure from their community by remaining silent.

In 1929 this opposition to government intervention, it should be known, was wholly nonpartisan. One of the largest of the Wall Street operators was John J. Raskob. He was also Chairman of the Democratic National Committee. So far from calling for preventive measures, Raskob in 1929 was explaining how, through stock market speculation, anyone could and should be a millionaire. Nor would the press have been enthusiastic about, say, legislation to control holding companies and investment trusts or to give authority to regulate margin trading. The financial pages of many of the papers were riding the boom. Never before or since had they been such exciting reading or had such an excited audience.

In short, all of the allies of the President were opposed, either by temperament or self-interest, to any action that might have anticipated or tempered disaster. Under these circumstances it is almost impossible to imagine that Coolidge or Hoover could have taken effective preventive action. They would have had to break with the community of which they were an intrinsic part.

Yet another President in another context might have been able to act. Many congressmen in these years were exceedingly critical of the Wall Street speculation and the corporate thimble-rigging. The liberal Republicans — the men whom Senator George H. Moses called the Sons of the Wild Jackass — were especially vehement. And so were more conservative figures such as Carter Glass. These men correctly sensed that things were going wrong. A President such as Wilson or either of the Roosevelts — the case of Theodore is less certain than that of Franklin — who was in turn surrounded in his cabinet by such men, would have been sensitive to their criticism. As a leader he would both have reinforced it and drawn strength from it for the necessary action. He might thus have arrested the more destructive madness as it became recognizable. The resulting conflict with business, banking and the press would have dramatized the problem and the consequent action. The American government works far better — perhaps it only works — when the Federal Executive and influential business and the respectable press are in some degree at odds. Only then can we be sure that abuse or neglect, either public or private, will be given the notoriety that is needed. In the time of Coolidge and Hoover, the Federal Executive, business and the press were united. These are the times in our democracy when all looks peaceful and much goes wrong.

I would not insist that by effective and timely criticism and action, the result of less concentrated power and influence, the Great Depression could have been avoided. Much was required in those days to make the United States in any degree depression-proof. But perhaps, by timely preventive action on speculation, the holding companies, and the payments balance, the ensuing depression might have been made less severe. If so, in the years following, the travail of bankers and businessmen before Congressional Committees, in the Courts and before the bar of public opinion, would have been less severe.

Here then is the great paradox. In the full perspective of history, American businessmen never had enemies as damaging as the men who grouped themselves around Calvin Coolidge and supported and applauded him in what William Allen White called "that masterly inactivity for which he was so splendidly equipped." Their best friends would have been men whom, for advocating timely action, they then would have considered their most dangerous enemies.

In arranging the management of the United States, Providence seems to have made no concessions to simplicity.

VII

The Build-up and the Public Man

IN LONDON a few years ago, a notable public career came
abruptly to an end, and the manner of its doing so has
meaning for every person in public life. By artifice and
imagination a personage of modest attributes had been re-
cast into historic, indeed immortal image. When the public
found out it had been fooled, it reacted precisely as one
might expect. Awe and admiration changed to calumny and
contempt. It did not matter that the individual was without
blame. It was he, and not the friends who had engineered
the false image, who suffered. It is always so.

My reference is to the Piltdown Man, called by some
Eoanthropus, who, it was discovered, had been given a personality he unmistakably did not possess. He had been
credited with being five hundred thousand years old and,
in prototype, one of the fathers of mankind. It was discovered that, in fact, he was only fifty thousand years old
and that his jaw was that of a modern ape with dentures.
Fifty thousand years is still a decent age for a skull; it is
sufficient to insure a moderately distinguished place in a
local museum. But Piltdown's friends were not satisfied;
they had given him a further build-up and, as regularly

happens to public figures, this accomplished his eventual ruin.

There is comfort for Americans in observing that Piltdown's build-up, and subsequent downfall, occurred in England. It shows that this is not exclusively an American phenomenon. Nevertheless, there can be little doubt that egregious exaggeration of the stature of the public figure is much more intimately a part of our political system than that of other countries, at least in the democratic world. Only with us does it have major political consequences. The time has come when the build-up, along with the two-party system, the primaries and the conventions, should be examined as an integral feature of our political life.

2

As noted, the build-up consists in giving a public figure a character which, in fact, he doesn't have. It has two forms, and, since the political scientists to date have been cautious in dealing with the phenomenon, they are still without names. There is first what may be called the *contrived* build-up. Secondly, there is the *autonomous* build-up. The categories are not mutually exclusive.

The contrived build-up is the best understood. As the name suggests, it consists in synthesizing a public reputation as a matter of deliberate design. In almost all cases — in this respect Piltdown was an exception — the individual himself is a party to the effort. In some instances he underwrites the cost. More often it is a deductible expense.

The contrived build-up is a notable phenomenon in our time and much attention is being given to its technique.

But it is also somewhat self-limiting in its effect. The man who hires a public relations man to impress the public with his intelligence, the dynamic qualities of his personality, or the depths of his devotion to the public good is tolerably recognizable as a man who hires a public relations firm to do these things. The same operation when undertaken less professionally by friends or associates does not gain in subtlety. There are many reasons why individuals will unite to proclaim the genius and beneficence of a third party, and in none of them is self-interest wholly lacking. There is nothing, not even Communism, which as a people we are so skilled at suspecting. Moreover, those who set out to give the build-up to a friend are rarely the kind of people who are reticent as to either their methods or their motives. They are likely to have an extrovert pride in both.

Yet the contrived build-up is not without importance or danger. It cannot be entirely good to have considerable industry devoted to the bamboozlement of the many about the merits of the few. In Washington during World War II, it was often observed that the man who came in with a factitious plea for higher prices or a larger allocation of scarce materials usually had a better prepared case than the honest petitioner and, on occasion, did rather better for himself. There is the chance that one of these days we will achieve contrived personalities that are superior in popular appeal to genuine ones. Perhaps there have already been examples. Then whether we elect or appoint boobs or good men to office will be a matter of random choice. Still, if recent experience is a guide, we have more to fear from the kind of build-up in which the element of contrivance, though usually not absent, is comparatively small. To this second type, the autonomous build-up, I now turn.

3

The autonomous build-up always strikes someone who is already in the public eye. Perhaps he has earned a measure of public esteem for doing an important and difficult job in a restricted area of public endeavor. Or he has made a promising start on such a job. Or, in a common case, he has just assumed public office after a respectable private career. Then comes the build-up. He is a man transformed — indeed he is no longer a man but a superman. His eccentricities become the mark of a unique personality. His hobbies are the refreshment of an intense and active mind. His wife becomes a gracious, untiring, and selfless partner. If he has had several wives, he has been tried by sadness. If he is a teetotaler, this marks him as a stern, disciplined and dedicated man. If he is given to belting the bottle, it will be said that he is not lacking in warmth and human qualities. But most remarkable of all are his qualifications for the job he has assumed. Where others ponder, he has solutions. That is because he is able to separate the essentials from the nonessentials and then find a painless course of action by shooting straight for the target. It has been the fault of lesser men that they had left the impression that there was a choice only between equally grim alternatives.

In fact, the build-up is particularly likely to occur at a time when problems are numerous, vexatious and incomprehensible. Not knowing how to control nuclear energy, disarm, increase needed expenditures, balance the budget, eliminate farm surpluses and come abreast of the Russians in space exploration, we find it desirable to invent people who can do these things. The press and networks, sensitive as always to the needs of the customer, assist. Working with whatever material is at hand, they create the master statesman who will see us through.

Such statesmanship, as a career, is not especially secure. The job turnover is very high. That is because, while it is easy to place a man on a pedestal, it is not at all easy to keep him there. A pedestal is a peculiarly public place. Since the build-up is indiscriminate in its selections, some rather grievous shortcomings may thus be revealed. And they are revealed, in the nature of the build-up, to a public whose expectations are inordinately high.

4

The years of the Great Depression and the war were ones of many troubles and a time when the build-up could be seen at its best — or most dangerous. It was F.D.R.'s personal good fortune that rather less was expected of him than of most Presidents coming to office. (Lippmann had dismissed him as qualified only by his desire for office.) But his assistants were soon involved in the perils of the build-up. For a short space of time in 1933, Raymond Moley, as a special envoy to the London Economic Conference, was the man on whom world economic policy seemed to turn. That one man should be the custodian of such stunning power and with the capacity to use it to such beneficent ends seemed impossible. It soon developed that it was impossible. The build-up carried Hugh Johnson to dizzy heights and to disaster. It made Donald Richberg an assistant president and a greater figure than Colonel House — temporarily. James A. Farley was for a time the greatest political magician since Metternich. As often happens, it is doubtful if the victim remained unpersuaded. His lofty attitude toward Roosevelt, whom history is likely to count the better man, was one unfortunate result. As the war approached, Knudsen, Stettinius, and Nelson were, in turn, the men who could be counted upon to arm the Republic in little time and at minimum inconvenience. All suffered for their failure to perform in accordance with an impossible promise of the build-up. In these years Henry Wallace, a good scientist and effective Secretary of Agriculture, became by the build-up a liberal Messiah of transcendent world vision. Although the build-up is a thing of peculiar danger to any conservative in whom great respectability is unmatched by great ability, it is not exclusively a menace to the right.

The New Deal also included one of the comparatively rare individuals who recognized the build-up as such and for what it could do to a man. In his diary, Harold Ickes tells how concerned he was when the build-up struck his character and integrity. The trouble with being Honest Harold, he observed, was that it made him a sitting duck for any showing of less than total rectitude. Plainly, he spent a fair amount of time wondering what chinks there might be in his armor and fearing that the *Chicago Tribune* would find them. How much better not to be billed as a paragon of honesty.

5

The problems which faced the Eisenhower Administration, in their own venue, were as puzzling as those with which Roosevelt had to deal. And they were attacked, uniformly, by conservatives. Nothing is more agreeable than to imagine that difficult problems are being solved by the right people. While it will use any available material, the press obviously prefers to work with Republicans. As a result, the build-up has worked havoc on the people who served with Ike.

The leading victim, without question, was the first Secretary of Defense, Charles E. Wilson. There is no empirical proof that he was a seriously worse secretary than his predecessors or successors in office. The faults of the Pentagon — the overblown bureaucracy, the flagrant rivalries, the inadequate technical performance — existed before he arrived and were worse only in degree after he departed. Yet Mr. Wilson's reputation as one of the more inadequate public figures of modern times would seem to be reasonably secure and not something on which there is likely to be petty partisan disagreement.

In part this was because he was a colorful figure in an otherwise colorless administration. And alone among his colleagues, he had the ability to say the wrong thing and drive home the point with an epigram that would command attention. So he is remembered for his references to the good of General Motors, to bird dogs and kennel dogs, to basic research being when you don't know what you are doing and for other memorable lines, actual or ascribed.

But he was also the victim of the build-up. The head of the nation's largest industrial corporation had become the head of its largest bureaucracy. The press reacted with unparalleled excitement. Miracles became inevitable — with Wilson there would be speeding up, cutting down, expediting, elimination of fat, a new sense of purpose, a total elimination of red tape. No one seems to have inquired whether presiding over General Motors was a natural preparation for these tasks or even whether they were capable of being accomplished at all. The build-up does not dwell on trifles. It having been said that Mr. Wilson would work miracles, it remained only to await the miracles.

When the miracles did not appear, the fault was put squarely on Wilson's shoulders. There is a convention which allows those who have taken part in the build-up to participate actively in the ensuing deflation. In this case, *Time,* which had greeted Wilson's appointment, like that of the Eisenhower cabinet in general, as a decisive forward step in the history of Western civilization, was a few months later deploring its hero's ignorance of "basic U.S. defense policies, or the strategic and historical considerations behind them" and was complaining further of his "unwavering refusal" to change his mind. The build-up had now gone into its drastic reverse phase. It rarely lets its man off at his point of departure. When working with ordinary efficiency, it leaves him well below zero.

The build-up has been only slightly less damaging to other members of the Eisenhower Administration. The terrible disaster that befell Robert T. Stevens, when he undertook the unrewarding task of trying to appease Joe

McCarthy, might have been less severe had he not previously been pictured as one of the Administration's vigorous, cleancut and dynamic young men. Mr. Benson's disesteem among farmers might have been milder if he had not been billed from the beginning as a man who would solve the farm problem on terms satisfactory to everyone. But perhaps the greatest sufferer was the President himself.

6

There is something about a general which makes him peculiarly susceptible to the build-up — the uniform gives him a certain added support and he has no civilian record which may seem to suggest an absence of genius. (Men like Harold Stassen are well protected against the build-up.) The wartime record which is now almost excessively complete shows that Dwight D. Eisenhower was an able umpire of interallied conflict. He maintained agreeable relations with some of the world's most self-centered men. And he managed to sustain among them the impression that Hitler was a proper object of their animosity. He was not, it would appear, a remarkable soldier but a remarkable soldier could have done much worse.

However, as the war continued, the build-up struck Eisenhower and then and thereafter it provided him with a Renaissance stature. He became a wise and perceptive philosopher of the homelier sort. It was believed that he would be an accomplished educator. He was assumed to have a sure-footed grasp of foreign policy. He was endowed with a feeling for politics without the reputation of being a politician. On domestic problems he was assumed to have

the kind of unspecific wisdom which makes all hard questions susceptible to sound solutions. Such was the Eisenhower build-up. Some of it, perhaps, was contrived for
political purposes. Much, much more was of the purely autonomous sort.

Very soon after he took office the period of disillusion set
in. Faithful readers of his press conference transcripts began
to whisper to each other that he was not a genius — that
he lacked the pervasive grasp of fact and logic which marks
the average news commentator. Visitors from the farm belt
learned with horror that he was not completely at home with
the question of farm price supports. So also with social
security and TVA. He had a previously unpublicized preference for golf.

On the record there is nothing surprising about this. The
army, like business or entomology, is a specialized career.
The President had never billed himself as a man of wide-
ranging intellectual curiosity; he had made a small point of
his preference for Westerns as reading matter. He had
never done battle over unions, social security, or the deficit.
Parity was not an issue around SHAEF. Nevertheless it was
the President and not those who gave him the bogus image
who was held to account. On this the build-up was as ever
insistent. He will be known as a President who fell far
short of his promise and it will be because the promise was
fantastic.

7

There may be no antidote to the build-up. Certainly personal modesty is not a secure defense. The general who

tries to arrest the inflation by saying "I'm just a plain soldier" will only cause those who are giving him the build-up to point out that, in addition to being a genius, he has a Godfrey-like humility. The businessman who protests, "The only thing I understand is production and more production," marks himself as a man who understands everything but won't say so. There was the recent case of Adlai Stevenson. He surely understood the perils of the build-up. At any rate, he set a new high standard for self-deprecation. His modesty served only to win him some of the most immodest hero worship of recent times. Perhaps he was saved from troublesome personal consequences of this, though not by any narrow margin, by the even bigger Eisenhower build-up.

Although there is no clear remedy for the build-up, it might help were we to resolve to remember that in a democracy leaders, at their best, are only the first among near-equals. So they will always share the bafflement of their followers. To build extravagant images of their wisdom renders no more service than the other modern habit of freely asserting their total venality. If we foster great expectations, we must count on deep disillusion.

VIII

The Nature of Social Nostalgia

Nᴜᴍᴇʀᴏᴜs mechanical contrivances — the square-rigged ship, the steam locomotive, the village pump, the spinning wheel — have the capacity to inspire nostalgia. Except in rare instances, and then usually as an expensive manifestation of personal idiosyncrasy, this nostalgia for earlier and usually simpler techniques does not lead to any serious effort to revive them. Much though we may prefer the extrovert and gushing personality of the steam locomotive to the silent, inward-turning, and incomprehensible Diesel, we do not urge a return to steam.[1] In social matters, by contrast, nostalgia for earlier arrangements leads regularly to the conclusion that they are better and that they should, if possible, be reinstated. This is not identified with any particular set of political attitudes. The social attitudes of both liberals and conservatives are deeply conditioned by social nostalgia. Some of the sharpest political conflicts of our time are between liberals who seek change to a nostalgic goal and conservatives who defend the status quo.

---

[1] India, since Gandhi, has indeed had to contend with a widespread demand that machine spinning and weaving be abandoned or greatly curtailed and that the spinning charkha and the handloom be rehabilitated. This reflects a nostalgia so profound as to have acquired the character of a religious drive.

The institutions which are the subject of nostalgia extend to the earliest and most archaic forms of social organization. One of the most interesting cases is the administration of both production and consumption by the household. The example is worth examining briefly.

2

In our cultural tradition the first agency for the general organization of production was the household. The latter was coextensive, more or less, with a family, ordinary or extended, but it might include some added hands. It was presided over by a patriarch (or more rarely a matriarch) who assigned the tasks, supervised the work, and undertook the more demanding tasks of craftsmanship or relations with the outside world. The family head also regulated the consumption of the household. Guided by tradition or individual contribution or need, he parceled out the fruits of efforts and controlled such stocks as it might be possible to accumulate against some later day of misfortune.

For the administration of consumption the household — perhaps now rather more matriarchal than of old — still serves. In the cultural tradition of the West, alternatives are hard to find. The highly socialized consumption of the Israeli *Kibbutz* is one of the few. In contrast, for organizing and administering production the household long ago showed itself to have severe limitations. The labor and capital supply available to it set a highly restrictive limit on the size of operations. Especially after the introduction of mechanical power, this was far too small for maximum efficiency. Production, therefore, was removed from the household to the factory. This reorganization reached massive proportions in the late eighteenth and early nineteenth century and earned the title of the Industrial Revolution. No institution can lose such an important part of its functions and not lose importance. Cottage industry gave to the family and home and the village life of pre–Industrial Revolution England an identity and a prestige which it has never since enjoyed. Goldsmith's Auburn owed its distinction to the fact that its houses were not only dormitories but workshops.

Much of the increased physical well-being of modern times we owe to the factory — to the divorce of production from the household. Had production remained a family enterprise, production per person could have increased only within narrow limits. The average person would at best be only marginally less poor than in England of the mid-eighteenth century. In the early years of the Industrial Revolution, life in the new industrial towns of England was singularly unpleasant. The towns were dark and dirty, and so were the houses. The toil was monotonous, and it endured incredibly for young and old alike. However, the factories have since improved and so have the towns. The hours are far less and the pay is far better. And the cottage industries which the factory system replaced had an evil side. Hunger can be a terrible taskmaster. To force a parent to drive his children like galley slaves, lest otherwise all starve, is not conducive to a happy family relationship. In Kashmir which in the brilliance and variety of its products is one of the world's last great centers of household industry, children of eight or ten spend twelve or fourteen hours a day at the wracking labor of the handloom. They may work under the benevolent eye of their parents, but they earn only meager food and a few rags, and their bodies are wasted by hunger and tuberculosis. It is unlikely that the household industry of Western Europe before the Industrial Revolution was much more attractive. In our own time homeworkers, most notably in the needle trades, have been the most exploited members of economic society. For a long time the very term "homework" was synonymous with weakness and industrial oppression and misery.

Yet the household as a comprehensive economic unit in charge of both production and consumption has never lost its hold on our thoughts. It inspires even our reverence. We can find many examples once we learn to recognize them. One largely (though not totally) harmless manifestation of this social nostalgia is the store that we set by handicraft manufactures of all kinds.

Handicraft products — handmade implements, hand weaving, carved bric-a-brac, pottery, glass, grass mats, hats, utensils — are sometimes rich in aesthetic functionalism. A country wisely protects and cherishes such an artistic tradition. It can also be profitable, for prices can reflect not cost but charm. As often, handicrafts are of unimaginative and stereotyped design, crude workmanship, low utility, and repulsive appearance. But merely because they are handicrafts, they are endowed with the virtues of the economic organization whence they come. They carry with them the aura of a family around a hearth, diligently at work under the eye not of a harsh foreman but a righteous parent. Given this endowment, their physical faults become virtues. Crudity is valued — to be able to detect the knife-marks of the carver or the fingermarks of the potter is good. The rough and repellent appearance is beauty. The person who fails to perceive their virtues is a cultural boor.

In the United States this interest in handicrafts rarely leads us to advocate a return to a handicraft industry. We recognize, at least implicitly, that it is costly and inefficient and that the returns are inherently meager. But we enthusiastically recommend handicraft industries to other people who are better conditioned to poverty. Economic missions to the underdeveloped countries regularly urge the revival of the "traditional" industries. It is a way of avoiding the steel mills and the power plants and the other heavy furniture of the Industrial Revolution. The Puerto Ricans have often been told to develop household industries at home rather than seek the higher incomes which an industrial order accords them in New York. Friends of the Navahos deeply deplore their tendency to desert their hogans and their blanket weaving and silversmithing for higher-paid industrial employment on the Atchison, Topeka and Santa Fe Railroad.

This manifestation of social nostalgia explains the unique reverence with which, in the United States, we regard the family farm. It is our most important surviving example of comprehensive economic administration by the household. Where, under the pressure of economic circumstance, the family farm gives way to a highly capitalized enterprise with a sizable labor force we do nothing about it. And almost any farm with less than a million dollars of invested capital or two airplanes can still be called a family farm.

But while farms do grow larger our verbal commitment to family administration remains complete. It provides virtu-

ous, diligent, and God-fearing parents with a unique opportunity to impress these commendable traits on their offspring.
Ignorant, shiftless, cruel, domineering, obscene, and incestu-
ous parents are imagined not to transmit these traits to
their offspring. In any case they are not part of the accepted
lore.

3

The household as an economic unit was supplemented by
small business enterprise — by the merchant who was in
command of his own capital, who employed his own servants
and agents, and who assumed personally the risks of buying and selling household products. Household manufacture itself gave way to the relatively small factory. Its owner
or his immediate agent directed the labor force, identified
himself with the product, assumed the risks of the business,
and took the profits. He was a simple and comprehensible
figure, and he had a straightforward role to perform. It
would have been surprising had he not also become the
object of social nostalgia, and he has. He is the small businessman.

There is no more distinctive feature of the modern industrial society than the great corporation. These have no single owner; management, direction, and achievement are
identified not with any individual but with an organization.
Perhaps these corporations suffer from a kind of social
elephantiasis. Size brings rewards in executive prestige, and
growth *qua* growth is the most obvious measure of executive
achievement. The distinction of heading the largest corporation far exceeds that of heading the most profitable cor-

poration. Yet we also owe the more distinctive achievements of modern capitalism to the large corporation. Certainly we are indebted to it for most of the goods by which we set such store. Automobiles, their gasoline, the electronic marvels, washing machines, refrigerators, the food that goes into them, bathtubs and the steel, copper, nickel, and aluminum from which or by which they are fabricated, all come from the vast organizations. The reason is simple. Instead of genius, the large corporation makes use of the combined efforts of many men of specialized but not remarkable ability. It substitutes organization for exceptional individual qualifications. This is highly efficient and something the small firm, by definition, cannot do. In addition the large corporation can command capital, minimize risk, and is a good vehicle for routine consumers' goods innovation.

The modern large corporation is not without defenders and friends. Some make its case without thought of compensation. Yet in the main it inspires only the affection that the small boy feels for the largest, strongest, or most homicidal of his contemporaries. Discretion, not love, is the ruling passion.

Small business, by contrast, is regarded with deep affection. Scholars, publicists, and politicians join in stressing its importance and viewing with alarm its prospects for survival. No one seriously argues that the small firm is ordinarily more efficient, more progressive, more responsible, more enlightened, that it pays better wages, or that it sells at lower cost than the large corporation. It is the object of social nostalgia.

This is not without consequences. American liberals have for many years devoted far more time and energy to regretting big business than to learning how best to live with it. Measures which might seem to limit the size and power of big business, most notably the enforcement of the antitrust laws, have evoked far more enthusiasm than measures to stabilize prices and wages and thus to temper the strong tendency to inflation which is all too obviously inherent in the price-making of powerful firms which deal, in turn, with strong unions. The practical consequences of nostalgic proposals to break up the large corporations are close to nil. Perhaps something can be done to limit growth or mergers but it is not clear that this changes much. While these nostalgic goals are being pursued more urgent problems that could be solved await action.

4

On occasion the influence of social nostalgia on events may be decisive. Thus, nothing is more deeply the subject of such nostalgia than the system of international exchange which the leading commercial countries of the world employed during the last century and for a brief period in the early part of the present century. Goods moved between countries as markets dictated. There were tariffs, but there were no quotas or other quantitative restrictions. National currencies were freely convertible into each other at rates which were fixed in turn by the fixed rates at which these currencies were convertible into gold. An American going to England in the last century (or buying British goods) knew with precise certainty that he could acquire a pound sterling for $4.86, and an Englishman knew with equal certainty that he would get as many dollars for a pound. There was no restriction whatever on the amount that could be so obtained; an Englishman could make loans in dollars or francs or marks secure in the knowledge that the number of pounds which he could acquire with these currencies would not have changed by the time his debt was repaid.

By the end of World War II little or nothing was left of these arrangements. Currencies had been cut loose from gold and from each other. Exchange values fluctuated. Usually there were several prices for the same currency, depending on the market in which it was bought and the legality of the transaction. Permission to acquire foreign currencies was strictly limited by most countries. So, consequently, was the freedom to trade and travel. It can hardly be wondered that men yearned nostalgically for the simplicity and the certainty of the former arrangements.

In the early postwar years, economic policy was deeply influenced by this nostalgia. In 1946 in the Anglo-American Financial Agreement (the British Loan) of that year, Britain was loaned $3.75 billion with the proviso that sterling would be made convertible on current account by mid-1947. In the nostalgic mood of the moment it was scarcely recognized that Britain was pursuing other, inconsistent, and almost certainly more important goals of economic and social policy. In 1925, under the guidance of Winston Churchill, then Chancellor of the Exchequer, Britain returned to a fixed rate of exchange between sterling and gold (and hence the dollar and other gold currencies) after a period of domestic inflation. At the fixed parity, British export prices were high.

They had to fall and they fell painfully. While they did so, there were wage cuts, unemployment, and great discontent. One consequence was the great general strike of 1926.

A different prospect was held out for the survivors of World War II. High and stable employment, stable prices, and a great expansion of social security were promised. These new goals inspired no nostalgia. But it would be hard to say that they were less important than prompt convertibility.

At the end of the war individuals, institutions, and governments in various parts of the world had large holdings of sterling. Should these be converted into dollars as, subject to some safeguards, would be possible with convertibility, British gold and dollar reserves would be drained away. To stop the drain, prices would have to fall drastically and wages be cut to reduce imports and consumption and make exports cheap. The consequences, as in 1925, would have been uncertainty, unemployment, and distress. Nevertheless, in Washington in 1946 social nostalgia scored a triumph. Convertibility was committed to a timetable. The consequences were fascinating and very costly.

In the summer of 1947, convertibility of sterling on current account was proclaimed on schedule. Drafts on the loan for essential imports had been heavy in the preceding months. Now alert possessors of pounds seized this God-given opportunity to be rid of their wartime accumulation of sterling and to acquire dollars or Swiss francs. International speculators saw a nearly certain opportunity for gain and bought or borrowed sterling to sell against dollars against the day when sterling would again be at a discount.

In the five weeks after convertibility was proclaimed, the British paid out about a billion dollars, in the main to such alert and fortunate people. By August 20, 1947, the loan, which had been meant to see Britain through the postwar years, was gone. Convertibility was suspended for another decade — until it could be reconciled with the nonnostalgic goals. To the British government and taxpayers remained the task of paying the interest on a loan that was wasted.

The aftermath was instructive. In Britain there was some criticism. Mostly, however, it centered on the failure of the Bank of England to detect promptly enough the drain of dollars and gold, and on the failure of the government to stop it. And the reaction was mild and soon forgotten. There was no scandal comparable with that which accompanied the much less costly efforts of the Labour government to develop large-scale production of peanuts for vegetable oil in Africa. In the United States there was no criticism at all, although the misguided disbursement by the government of several billion dollars for no useful purpose often attracts adverse comment. This experiment was nostalgic and hence noble.

5

In recent years our agricultural policy has been strongly influenced by social nostalgia. Until the creation of Herbert Hoover's Farm Board in 1929 and its subsequent stabilization operations, farm markets in peacetime were largely free of public control. The free market was never very much appreciated by farmers. It was a source of recurrent and devastating hardship resulting from violently adverse price movements. Many farmers sullenly regarded these price fluctuations as a form of exploitation. The explanation that they were part of the natural order of things, such as a virile economic man would welcome, never had a popular place in agrarian attitudes. Since the early thirties, farm prices have been subject to a considerable measure of intervention and control. These years, with exceptions, have been far happier for farmers. They have also been years of unprecedented technical advance in agriculture. While our industrial lead over the Soviet countries has been narrowed, our advantage in agricultural efficiency has almost certainly increased. Surpluses, troublesome as they may be, are a manifestation of this efficiency. The encouragement given by firm price supports to planning investment and inaugurating technical innovation has almost certainly been a factor in this advance. No other Western country — England, Canada, France, Germany, Sweden, or Switzerland — leaves its farmers to the strained mercy of the free market.

Agricultural policy continues, nonetheless, to be heavily influenced by the nostalgia for the free market. This existed in the past so it must exist again. Secretary of Agriculture Ezra Taft Benson, one of the more humorless public figures of the twentieth century, has come close, on occasion, to identifying the free market with divine ordinance. Little real attempt has been made to design a system of support prices that will work. This would not be an unduly difficult task. Instead, all effort has been concentrated on minor movements toward market freedom. These have accomplished nothing. On the contrary, they have served only to magnify the surpluses and the cost of accumulating and carrying them.

Social nostalgia supports the belief that the state governments are more desirable instruments of public administration than the Federal Government, although most recent experience would suggest that the Federal Government is usually the more efficient and effective, as well as more honest administrator, and that it is also generally more responsive to popular will. Nostalgia supports our hopeful confidence that all government can be small, that the government governs best by governing least; and that in a highly urbanized society, planning and guidance of growth can somehow be avoided. Nostalgia even forces campaigning Presidential candidates to whistle-stop into every corner of the country, for that once was necessary if people were to see whom they were selecting.

Finally, social nostalgia supports our continuing conviction that life can be simple and that difficult problems will yield to old and familiar rules and formulae. The family and the church will save us; we must have a simple faith for our times; we should be led by a simple man of simple beliefs. We stop just short of praise of the simple mind. Simplicity provides an important clue to social nostalgia.

6

In matters of social policy we are strongly partial to what we believe we understand. The institutions that are subject to social nostalgia belong to an earlier age. For that reason they are — or at least they seem to be — more uncomplicated, more understandable than what has taken their place.

The wagon maker is within ready reach of the mind; not so General Motors. The village is comprehensible but not New York.

More important, because an institution has existed it has been pondered. Theories have been woven as to its behavior; these have made it a part of the cultural heritage. By contrast, the institutions that have replaced it will for a time have no literature, no theory. They will not be studied, for there are no books to study. In comparison with the nostalgic institution they thus seem formless, incomprehensible, and alien. Currency convertibility has back of it the theory of international trade and of foreign exchange, the most sophisticated achievement of economics. It is detailed, rational, and complete. The exchange control to which Britain and other countries resorted pragmatically during World War II is described only in the official histories. Few would think of making a scholarly reputation by teaching and writing on its theory and practice. The advantage of the older way, of the known as against the unknown, is obvious. It may sustain it, as in the case of the convertibility clauses of the British Loan, in face of grave practical disadvantages.

Older institutions are not only comprehensible, but in the process of being made so they will have been idealized. Unpleasant or inconvenient features will have been dropped from sight. The price system is a case in point. Some prices were always fixed by monopoly, and still others by custom. Yet others, such as electric rates, have usually been fixed as the result of sundry political pressures, by state action. Some people, such as employers of labor, had a strong bargaining position. Others, such as those who worked for wages and without organization, were often very weak. Prices that were subject to the control only of competition of the market might, as the result of war, famine, or other catastrophe, move with punishing vigor. To make the system comprehensible, these irregularities were largely ignored; the ideal situation without such inconveniences was then assumed. The nostalgia is not for the reality but for this abstraction.

It is known that the palace of the great Louis at Versailles was notably deficient by any modern standards in its plumbing. Yet peristalsis in that noble and well-nourished court was normal. And the inevitable expedients led to a horrid stench everywhere about the glittering grounds. When the orangery was planted it was hoped, alas in vain, that its fragrance would overcome the terrible smell. All this has been lost in the idealization. Of the court of Louis XIV we know only of the pomp, the wit, and the love. Of features which would have made life there impossible for a fastidious American nothing is remembered. So with social nostalgia.

7

Lastly, social nostalgia owes much to the nature of social change. This, in the ordinary course of events, occurs under conditions of special difficulty. Institutions do not buckle in quiet and peaceful times; they fail under strain. It is always hoped that a return to normal times will bring back the earlier arrangements; sometimes it does. But sometimes the old institutions were fatally weak, and difficult times only exposed that weakness.

Also since the new institutions arrived in what seemed to be extraordinary times, they also seem to be extraordinary. They were the result of emergency measures, taken in emergency, and thus were meant to disappear when the emergency passes. But they don't. The old arrangements were due to go anyway and the emergency only sped the passing. Conservatives have long supposed that much permanent change appears in the guise of emergency action. They are right, and they are wrong only in thinking that someone so contrives matters.

Thus the world capital market broke down in the nineteen-thirties and was replaced by the United States government by a seemingly endless succession of emergency programs for the export of capital — the Export-Import Bank, Lend-Lease, UNRRA, Greek-Turkish Aid, Marshall Plan, Point IV, Mutual Security, Economic Aid. But not since before World War I had capital moved easily and reliably around the world. The system was ill adapted to a world of rising nationalism, incipient socialism, and recurrent military tension. Social nostalgia keeps the hope of the revival of an international capital market alive. We may reflect on how many emergency measures have become part of our normal way of life.

One reason that social nostalgia is not always, perhaps not usually decisive in action is that, ordinarily, it must operate against the clear dictates of circumstance. The nostalgic goal seems admirable in principle, but impossible or inconvenient in practice. Therefore, those who are in positions of responsibility, while proclaiming their devotion to the nostalgic goal, usually find it necessary to explain why they must postpone its pursuit. A goodly part of our political discussion, at any given time, is devoted to the praise of institutions which their proponents would not want if they could have them. The free price system, uninhibited competition, the renaissance of the states, the gold standard, and education based on the McGuffey Readers are all advocated by individuals who would be appalled were they to succeed. An interested desire to turn attention from more important things sometimes plays a role in this advocacy. But when we have learned to look, we shall regularly see the unremitting pressure of social nostalgia.

IX

Was Ford a Fraud?

I should like to say a special word about this piece on Ford. We have a tendency that is wholly familiar to place our heroes on a pedestal and accord them what is rightly called worship. And this hero worship as surely provokes the tendency for others to search for signs of clay feet, straw in the shirt, or a furtive twitch of the eye. Like the progressive income tax, these critics exert a leveling influence without which democracy might not survive. When Douglas MacArthur returned from Japan to his frenzied reception in 1951, he should have been told that the very tumult in the streets would be causing some very acute citizens to consider how his shortcomings might be better revealed. A picture on the cover of Time Magazine, *as any perceptive recipient of the honor must know, is taken by a large number of people to mean that the individual is henceforth much more in need of expert criticism than applause.*

However, this suspicion of heroic stature is no doubt most useful when directed at the living. It is also by way of being more fair. I have been concerned lest in attacking the Ford myth I seem to be debunking for the sake of debunking the reputation of a man now dead. This is not my intention. In recent times, Ford's former friends and associates, as well as histories based on the official records, have provided us with a mass of evidence that is inconsistent with much (though not all) of the Ford legend. They show Ford's exceptionally comprehensive shortcomings as an entrepreneur. They show that James Couzens, Ford's great

*partner, was a more nearly decisive figure in Ford's early for-
tunes than has been supposed or than Couzens himself bothered
to claim.*

*They show also that Ford was the product of a pioneer public
relations ploy. His world-famous industrial philosophy was man-
ufactured precisely as was the Model T save that with the
Model T, Ford had rather more to do with the design and
specifications. The producer was Samuel Crowther. Ford avidly
and enthusiastically abetted both this and other efforts to bemuse
the public. The public, it must be said, was highly acquiescent.*

*Since Ford's time public relations has become our youngest
profession. No great executive's personality or ideas are now released to the public without extensive retouching. We have made
our accommodation to this — although it is not one that is
entirely advantageous to the businessman. Not knowing what
to believe, we have resolved where the executive is concerned
to believe nothing. Were Leonardo to be installed tomorrow
as the president of General Motors, it would not be known for
many years. The press releases which said so, the things which
he would later say and write, the paintings he would paint and
the inventions that he would contrive would all be attributed to
some excessively inspired PR-man. It is distressing to discover
that the Ford myth is the first of the industrial fairy tales — not
in total, of course, but in considerable part. If we resolve, as we
must, that the purveyors of fiction and bamboozlement will not
get the better of us, then we must start right there.*

T HE LITERATURE of Ford and the Ford Motor Company
is rivaled in the world of business only by that of Rockefeller and Standard Oil, and in the last twenty-five years it
has been infinitely more interesting. It has passed through
three distinct phases: ecstatic, doubtful, and analytical.
Ford and his company became nationally and internation-
ally famous in 1914, the year of the five-dollar day. The

ecstatic phase lasted from then until 1929. During these years, the Ford literature was composed in a mood of nearly unalloyed wonder. Authors visited Highland Park, where the moving assembly line was born and which was the main center of manufacturing until the close of World War I, and thereafter the vast plant on the River Rouge, and their only problem was to find adjectives to fit the marvels. For many, the wonder was unquestionably heightened by the fact that these were the first manufacturing plants they had seen.

And if the plants were marvelous, so must be their owner, for no American businessman was more intimately identified with his enterprise than Ford. One needed to be told at least once that Rockefeller was Standard Oil. Ford was Ford. From almost the beginning, he owned a majority of the stock, and after 1919 he owned the whole company, lock, stock, and barrel. Rockefeller retired around the turn of the century although he lived for nearly another forty years. Until he was eighty, Henry Ford remained the most important man in the company he founded.

Ford himself was far from averse to this literature of acclaim. A onetime socialist named Allan L. Benson, who went to Dearborn in the early twenties to write a book, was agreeably surprised when Ford invited him to use his private office. "You can have a typewriter brought in and anything else you want." It was a good arrangement, for Ford was almost never in the office. And Benson was no man to bite the hand. "Mr. Ford sees the world in great disorder," he noted in a sample of the Ford prose of the period, "and his passion is to set it right . . . His mind is no longer solely concerned with the manufacture of automobiles. It is concerned with the infinitely greater problem of organizing the industrial world. Ford's brain is in the United States, but his thoughts roam throughout the universe."

Ford was himself, at least nominally, one of the largest sources of this approving literature. Although nothing in the Ford legend is better established than his rustic contempt for the man of words, he authored no fewer than three books in the twenties and very early thirties. Together they had a large circulation, and all spoke exceedingly well of Ford's accomplishments and intentions. And perhaps immodesty should not be hinted, for they were written to the last paragraph by Samuel Crowther. A few samples of Ford's real writing have survived in the form of letters. His syntax and spelling have many of the rough-and-ready qualities of the planetary transmission.

One may add that these books, apart from glorifying Ford, showed a virtuosity in devising, *ex post*, a rationale for earlier decisions that would have been impressive even to Mr. Dulles. Ford's ideas on the importance of keeping clear of the banks, on how to run a railroad, on mass production, on the moving assembly line, and on the five-dollar day were all formed and issued retrospectively. Ford did not deny that he was an empiricist, and he used to love to say: "We go forward without facts and we learn the facts as we go along." Charles Sorenson (not a hostile witness) has said that he should have added: "I have a hunch, and I'll have it put into words if it works out."

But this was said a long time later. In the great years, Ford's view of Ford was widely accepted at face value.

Even when Ford promised to rebate every cent of his profits on World War I production, everyone assumed he would do so. (A bit later he thriftily reneged, and no one noticed.)

Not that these years were without their sour notes. Ford's political adventures inevitably brought attack. The peace ship of 1915 was enthusiastically ridiculed, although possibly it was one of Ford's better buys in the field of ideas. To hope that men and women of good will might possibly mediate a conflict in which the generals had been reduced to marching their men against the machine guns in the hope that they would have a few survivors when the other side was all killed was natural if perhaps optimistic. In any case, no one had a better plan.

In these years also Ford tangled with predictable consequences with Colonel Robert R. McCormick. Ford was a pacifist. This was wounding to the Colonel in a war which (by his later rescript) he was to win all but singlehanded. The *Tribune* called Ford an "anarchist," and also an "ignorant idealist" although it is not on record that it ever recognized any other kind. Ford then made the hideous mistake of suing for libel, and the *Tribune* lawyers gleefully undertook to prove at least the ignorance. Questioned about the American Revolution, Ford remembered imperfectly that there had been one in 1812. He confused Benedict Arnold with an impeccably loyal Horace L., who had written a book about the company's shop practices. But these misfortunes did not greatly dim the image. Nor did his later adventures in anti-Semitism, in part because anti-Semitism was still practiced by the best people. Until the end of the twenties, Ford was the nation's most astonishing man.

2

In the depression the Ford literature changed. In 1929 Charles Merz published his *And Then Came Ford*,[1] a generally factual story of the company and the man. It was the first such history. After 1930, there was no more of Crowther's talented fiction. In the twenties, Ford had regularly promised either the incredible or the impossible — flivvers that would fly, pastoral factory towns, a magic wand over Muscle Shoals, farms devoid of drudgery and made prosperous by the sale of soybeans and straw. These things did not happen; but people were willing to believe they might, and so possibly was Ford. In the thirties, an age of disenchantment, these visions became less saleable. (However, as late as 1940, when the country was wondering if it could get any bombers in time, Henry Ford said he could easily get out a thousand a day.)

And presently there was a good deal of criticism. Men who were knowledgeable in the automobile business said that Ford was unprogressive — he had remained frozen too long to the obsolete Model T. The company, it was said, was losing ground rapidly to General Motors and Chrysler, and the good executives had been purged. Later came the charge that Harry Bennett and his private army had taken over.

In the years of the proletarian novel and the New Deal, much of the critical literature was frankly from the left. Ford was anti-union, and the company was one of the nation's leading exponents of the speed-up. But conserva-

[1] Garden City: Doubleday, 1929.

tive journals were also heard from. So were former Ford executives. And during the war, Ford and his company became a target. Instead of the thousand bombers a day from Willow Run, it looked as though there would be more nearly none. The government considered taking over, although eventually the bombers came.

In 1948 Keith Sward published his *The Legend of Henry Ford*.[2] The author's sympathies were plainly with Local 600 of the United Automobile Workers and not with Ford. But it was no shallow partisan tract. Sward dwelt in detail on Ford's shortcomings as an employer, a manufacturer, and as a person. It was a strong adverse case, and it profoundly affected the books that followed. For friendlier observers felt obliged to try to refute Sward's charges. And in doing so, they invariably confirmed enough of his case to show a very grave default.

But just as the earlier praise had discordant notes, so now the attack was salted with admiration. The legend of Ford benevolence received a severe pummeling. And so, toward the end, did the legend of Ford omnipotence. But no one, not even Sward, denied to Ford the credit for building the greatest industrial establishment of its day. The reputation of Ford the great entrepreneur — the man who was capable of first glimpsing opportunity and pioneering where others imitated — remained intact. He was a genius or at least an ex-genius.

Moreover, by the thirties and forties Ford had become a folk figure. He had helped with his unbelievable promises and also his impenetrable epigrams. "I never made a mis-

2 New York: Rinehart, 1948.

take, and neither did you." He also benefited from the nostalgic affection that was felt for his machine, the immortal Model T. The car had been a keystone of American humor. A man had asked that his Ford be buried with him. It had never failed to get him out of a hole. A farmer lost the tin roof of his barn in a windstorm. On advice he sent it to Detroit. Promptly back came the word, "Your car is one of the worst wrecks we have seen, but we will be able to fix it." The car and the man resembled each other. Both were spare, unadorned, and utilitarian. Both were individualists with more than a touch of eccentricity, and in both the eccentricity increased notably with age. In his *Farewell to Model T,*[3] Lee Strout White said in 1936: "The car is fading from the American scene — which is an understatement because to a few million people who grew up with it, the old Ford *was* the American scene." So was Ford, and for the same reason his performance could be very bad and yet be above serious reproach.

3

Finally in the literature of Ford have come the memoirs and the efforts at objective history. Numerous former Ford executives have been encouraged to tell what they remembered of the great days to a recording machine. Even such an improbably literary figure as Harry Bennett published his recollections, and a shocking number of them have been confirmed by his contemporaries. In 1956 the important memoirs of Charles E. Sorenson made their appearance.[4]

[3] New York: Putnam's, 1936.
[4] *My Forty Years With Ford.* New York: Norton, 1956.

Sorenson, Cast-Iron Charlie to the trade, survived longer in Ford's confidence as the top production executive than any other man. He was an able engineer and organizer and a superlative hatchet man. Although he deals somewhat sketchily with this latter talent, other Ford executives whose careers he ended have gone into it in respectful detail.

Finally, detailed histories of Ford are being written by Allan Nevins and Frank Ernest Hill. The first of these told the story up to World War I.[5] The second volume appeared in 1957 and dealt with the years in which the Ford Motor Company reached its zenith and then began to lose ground to its rivals.[6] Another at this writing is to come. Were we half as serious about capitalism and free enterprise as the liturgy of the luncheon speech proclaims, these books about the most famous of our corporations would be a landmark. They are superbly researched, and the writing is infinitely superior to the tendentious drivel in which the ordinary company history is offered. In my view, the picture of Ford which they seek to leave is neither right nor even wholly plausible. But if an acceptable view of Henry Ford ever gains currency, it will owe much to Nevins and Hill.

The problem posed by Nevins and Hill, and by all the Ford literature, is that Ford is presented as a genius — an eccentric genius to be sure — who fails to reveal his genius even on the matters where it is supposed to be sublime. The nature of Ford's greatness has been variously identified. Crowther and likewise William J. Cameron, long

[5] *Ford: The Times, The Man, The Company.* New York: Scribner's, 1954.
[6] *Ford: Expansion and Challenge, 1915–1933.* New York: Scribner's, 1957.

familiar as the Sunday night voice of Ford on the radio, credited their employer with total social, economic, political, and philosophical insight. This view was widely accepted. Ford's social insights — those that led him to high wages and the five-dollar-day and to the social benefits of mass production — are still very much a part of the myth.

Edison, who at first did not like Ford but later became his friend, is quoted as saying that "Ford is a 'natural businessman' just as he is a 'natural mechanic,' and he is the rarest of all types, in that he is a combination of the two." Certainly it is believed that Ford was the greatest business figure of his age and his mechanical genius is all but unchallenged. Nevins and Hill, who are more cautious about the qualifications of their hero than most, think his mechanical ability was beyond compare.

But if Ford had such vast endowments in these different fields, why was his performance in each marked by obtuseness and stupidity and, in consequence, by a congeries of terrible errors, many of them later admitted? Let us examine the record, beginning with Ford's performance as a political and social leader and as a philosopher.

In politics Ford was erratic and incompetent and, despite his vast industrial reputation, a disastrous failure. In 1918 he ran for the Senate on the Democratic ticket; and in 1924 he was, for a time, bitten by the presidential bug. Neither of these forays did anything to disprove his own candid observation that "about politics as a business I know nothing at all," or the acid suggestion of the *New York Times* that his election in 1918 "would create a vacancy both in the Senate and in the automobile business." In his campaign Ford made no speeches, most likely because he could not speak. His most memorable contribution to political thought was the hint that, if elected Senator, he would take the Ford organization to Washington to help him. Reminded during his senatorial campaign of an earlier boast that he had rarely bothered to vote, he let it be known that in 1884, just turned twenty-one, he had gone promptly to the polls and on his father's advice marked his ballot for President Garfield. That was three years after Garfield was assassinated. (Ford had other such accidents. From the peace ship went a cable to Pope Benedict VII, who died in 983.) In this campaign Ford was for Wilson and the League of Nations. But this alignment with the angels must be set against later flirtations with such unrewarding figures as Father Coughlin, Fritz Kuhn, and Gerald L. K. Smith. And common political shrewdness, if nothing else, would have warned him against *The Protocols of the Wise Men of Zion*, a notorious forgery, and the other racial rubbish that month after month appeared in the *Dearborn Independent*, along with Mr. Ford's own page, and which blamed the Jews for all man's sins and most of his misfortunes since Moses. When, in the end, the popular, commercial, and legal objections to this farrago became overpowering, Ford set a new standard for audacious falsehood by denying that he had had anything to do with it. "Had I appreciated even the general nature, to say nothing of the details, of these utterances, I would have forbidden their circulation without a moment's hesitation." [7] The denial was not only bogus but foolish. Every person whose knowl-

[7] From Ford's retraction in 1927 following settlement of his lawsuit with Aaron Sapiro. Quoted in Nevins and Hill, *Expansion and Challenge,* p. 321.

ledge counted knew that Ford had been specifically and personally responsible.

Ford's formal economic and social philosophy was also bogus. There is full agreement with Sorenson that it was worked out after the fact by Crowther and presented to Ford for his approval. The public was here the victim of one of the first operations of the public relations man. But where nowadays it would be assumed that such views had been concocted by a PR firm and discounted accordingly, then the public was not so experienced in mendacity. Ford got credit for thinking up what he said.

It will be suggested that acts, not the subsequent theory from Crowther, were what counted — they reflected an unarticulated but compelling wisdom, and this was Ford's. But here too there is question. Mass production — elaborately synchronized manufacture, flow and assembly of parts and components and product — was no doubt carried farther at Highland Park in the second decade of the century than in any other plant in the world. But this was a development, not an invention. Ideas were borrowed from dozens of other establishments of the day. The Ford engineers and managers were forced to improvise and experiment because of the relentless demand for cars. The borrowing, improvisation, and experiment were done by many men. Ford's own role was certainly no greater than that of several others, and it could have been less. The most spectacular of the Ford contributions to mass production was the steadily moving assembly line. Of this, Sorenson avers, Ford, so far from being the inventor, was for a long time a skeptic.

A number of the more critical authors like Sward, and even the friendly Roger Burlingame,[8] attribute the five-dollar day to James Couzens. Couzens was seeking, they argue, by one brilliant stroke to stop an excessive labor turnover and solve the main problem of the time which was how to get out more cars. The evidence is not decisive. The idea was apparently mooted at a conference at the plant held either on New Year's Day, 1914, or the following Sunday. It is at least possible that the proposal came from Ford and that he was encouraged to offer it because of the profits the company was making. (In 1913 the company had netted $27 million on sales of around $100 million.) And in any case, Ford was in charge, and this kind of decision (as distinct from a general engineering development like mass assembly) ought to be credited to the man who was the boss.

However, it doesn't greatly matter, for Ford was a high wage employer for only a few years. He was not sufficiently convinced of the high wage philosophy to avoid becoming one of the most unsatisfactory employers in town. For a long time in face of the World War I inflation, Ford wages remained the same; by the early twenties when the Ford minimum had been raised to $6, other companies were paying regular labor as much and skilled workers more. Meanwhile Ford's car was obsolete but Ford was convinced that people would buy it if only the price was low enough. The price was indeed low — a Ford roadster cost $290 f.o.b. Detroit in 1926 — and so were costs. These were brought down by taking it out of the men. Sorenson and his asso-

[8] *Henry Ford: A Great Life in Brief.* New York: Knopf, 1955.

ciates were the masters of the speed-up. In 1914 the Highland Park plant was no doubt a pleasant and remunerative place to work. By the mid-twenties the River Rouge, by even the most friendly evidence, was a machine-age nightmare. Recalling the early twenties, William C. Klann, one of the ablest of the older Ford executives, said a trifle repetitively: "We were driving them, of course. We were driving them in those days . . . Ford was one of the worst shops for driving the men." The driving continued until 1941 when the United Automobile Workers, CIO, finally organized Ford, the last of the auto makers to yield. By then wages, and more particularly working conditions, in the home of the five-dollar day were markedly substandard. Ford Local 600 would long be a center of turbulence and left-wing influence. It was partly because its members had experienced at first hand Ford's wage and labor philosophy.

In the early years of the five-dollar day, Ford's welfare programs for his workers had merit. The famous Sociology Department helped immigrant workers to learn English and to protect themselves from the many thieves who sought their pay checks. But paternalism, as so often, degenerated into petty interference and even tyranny, and Ford's own ideas, as distinct from those of the professional social workers, seem to have been principally at fault. Ford was greatly opposed to his workers having male boarders in their houses. Evidently no wife was really to be trusted. He conducted a relentless and humiliating crusade against the use of alcohol and tobacco. In the twenties, a Ford deliveryman in Omaha, when offered a cigarette for some courtesy, asked with obvious embarrassment if he could keep it until evening. He dared not smoke on duty. When the depression came and the breadlines lengthened, Ford's social vision allowed him to conclude that these were "wholesome" and "the best times we ever had."

4

Neither was Henry Ford a businessman.

On this the evidence is decisive, and if there is any uncertainty as to what a businessman is, he is assuredly the things Ford was not.

Ford paid no attention to questions of company organization — there usually wasn't much after Couzens left — or to administration, costs, marketing, customer preference, or (at least by his own assertion) profits. The older executives at the Ford Motor Company agree that power was not delegated but appropriated. In the late thirties and early forties, Harry Bennett carried this technique to the logical conclusion by basing his authority on armed force. Balance sheets and cost accounts meant nothing to Henry Ford. Neither did his dealer organization, although when Model T ceased to sell, he blamed it on the dealers. One of his contributions to the merchandising of Ford cars was to ban advertising for several years. Some will insist that he had the greatest of all business talents, which was a sure feel for what the customer wanted. Perhaps he did, but not reliably so. In the twenties, he failed to see that people, new car buyers at least, wanted a more comfortable and elegant car than he was providing and would pay for it. He stuck with the Model T and surrendered the leadership of the industry to General Motors. He is remembered for saying that the customers could have Model T in any color "so long as it is black." This was refreshing individualism and so much a part of Ford's character that Will Rogers, taking cognizance of Ford's presidential ambitions in the early twenties, offered him an unbeatable slogan: "Voters, if I'm elected, I'll change the front." But it was supreme indifference to those he was supposed to serve, and it nearly ruined the company.

A considerable part of Ford's business reputation traces to his success in 1919 in buying out the minority stockholders (for a total of $105,820,894.57) and then in 1920–21, when the postwar depression came, in saving the company from the influence of the bankers from whom he had borrowed money to buy the stock.[9]

These transactions may have been shrewd. To some sensitive souls, they might have overtones of blackmail. Whether they were good business is much less clear. The minority stockholders were first softened up for the sale by cutting the dividends on their Golconda, which had previously been vast, to a purely nominal amount. (There was some reason for this because the Dodge Brothers, who held a minority interest, were using Ford revenues to build up their own automobile company.) Then when the courts ordered Ford to resume dividend payments, he let it be known that he was leaving the company (Edsel had recently replaced him as president) and would soon, through another firm, bring out a new, better, and much cheaper

---

[9] Ford received a credit of $75,000,000, not all of which was used, from Chase Securities Corporation, the securities affiliate of the Chase National Bank, the Old Colony of Boston, and Bond and Goodwin of Boston.

Ford. After this remarkably disquieting news had had a chance to sink in — some speak of despair and panic among the stockholders — Ford representatives came along with an offer. This was handsome. Most of the Ford stock was purchased for $12,500 a share, up, in a matter of fifteen years, from $100. Then, of course, no more was heard of the new company or the new car.

The company was "saved" from the bankers by equally compelling methods. When car sales fell off in 1920 and left Ford with his debt and an expensive inventory of materials and parts, he had the inventory converted into Model T's. These were then consigned in volume to the dealers, who had the choice of getting the money or getting out of the business. Most of them got the money. Ford's debt was transferred from himself to his thousands of dealers. More precisely, the banks, friends, relatives and in-laws of the dealers paid off Ford's creditors in New York and Boston. They did it reluctantly and sometimes with fury in their hearts.

But what did Ford gain? The company could have reached an arrangement with the banks and the slump soon passed. Everyone has since believed that the banker influence would have been inimical, but few have paused to consider that General Motors, which was by no means a stranger to such influence, did not suffer. On the contrary, in the immediately ensuing years this banker-influenced company forged far ahead of the Ford Motor Company. Actually the notion that the bankers were a disaster was the invention of Henry Ford, who propagated it sedulously to the whole world.

What Ford won by these coups was the autocratic power which was nearly to ruin him. In the process he had bought out a genuinely talented businessman to whom his debt was enormous. This was James Couzens.

Until 1915 the Ford Motor Company, as a business, was run by Couzens.[10] He set up the dealer organization, managed sales, bought materials and parts, approved capital outlays, enforced cost discipline, kept the books, watched the earnings, and held and paid out the money. He was a superb organizer, and he had a brilliant sense for both large issues and small. His later career in politics — he was police chief and mayor of Detroit and as a Roosevelt Republican he eventually got the Senate seat for which Ford was defeated — showed that he was a man of versatile intelligence. And he was not Ford's man. Couzens was a part owner and junior partner. Though he admired his senior partner, he once said that he would work with Henry Ford but not for him. One clue to the Ford mystery, on which I shall say a word presently, is that the company ran into troubles that became chronic very soon after the departure of Couzens.

5

A visitor to Ford's office in the twenties was interested to observe a half life-size picture of the Prince of Wales, the present Duke of Windsor. "I met him twice when he was over here," Ford told his visitor. "I think he is the hope of England." Ford's judgment of business talent was no

---

[10] Cf. Harry Barnard, *Independent Man: The Life of Senator James Couzens.* New York: Scribner's, 1958.

better. The worst of his selections, of course, was Harry Bennett. The latter, along with his satellite prizefighters, punks, ex-football players (and Coach Harry Kipke after he had been relieved at Ann Arbor) and assorted baccalaureates of the Michigan penal institutions, eventually made the Ford Motor Company into an industrial charnel house. And Harry was Henry's boy. Everyone, including Bennett himself, agrees that Ford, so far as treating him like his own son, treated him far better.

But more noteworthy than Ford's disposition to select the wrong man was his penchant for firing the right ones. Under his leadership, the history of the company became one of endless purges and resignations. Couzens, Knudsen, Wills, Hawkins, Rockelman, the Lelands of Cadillac and Lincoln, Klingensmith, Kanzler — the list goes on and on. These were not superannuated bureaucrats. Most of them were in their prime, and with rare exceptions they were grabbed up by General Motors, by Chrysler when it came along, or by one of the smaller rivals. Those who went to Chrysler and General Motors had the pleasure of helping their new employers end Ford's leadership of the industry.

As time passed, Ford took delight in speeding his departing help with devious sadistic gestures. Men discovered they had been fired when they learned that their office furniture had been moved out or, as on one occasion, when their desks were chopped up with an axe. However, quite a few got the bad news with unadorned Scandinavian bluntness from Charles E. Sorenson, who at the end of World War II, like Robespierre, knelt under his own knife. The delay in getting out Model A and the poor wartime and postwar performance could readily be traced to Ford's unwillingness to have around him men of ability and wisdom. "The spirit of the factory after 1920," Nevins and Hill observe, "was not stimulating, but repressive." The same could unquestionably be said of the front office.

So much for Ford's executive development program.

6

Ford also had appalling shortcomings as a mechanic.

This will be the most difficult to swallow, and not alone by those unlearned in the Ford lore. Nevins and Hill say flatly that "as a mechanical genius he was perhaps the greatest of his time." Not even the most hostile commentators disagree. But those who use these phrases do not pause to reconcile them with Ford's mechanical performance which they also chronicle.

First as to Ford's formal qualification, he seems to have had no knowledge of chemistry, physics, or mathematics. Instead, he was given to wild fantasies on scientific matters such as his conviction that meals should be so ordered that starches, proteins, and fruit acids should not be mixed.

Nor was he qualified in the simple techniques of the engineer's and designer's trade. Few things have been more debated than whether Ford could read a blueprint. But if he could, he wouldn't. His method, if such it could be called, was wholly empirical — to cut and try.

If one supposes that a man can be a great painter or a great composer without knowledge or study of his art, then just conceivably one can be a great mechanic as the fruit of pure inspiration. (It is harder in the case of mechanical genius to dismiss knowledge of the underlying science, past experience and even the elementary tools of the trade.) But there will surely be doubts about the inspiration of, say, the composer who, in his orchestration, refuses to shake a childhood predilection for the kazoo. Such was the case with Ford.

Until nearly the last Model T came off the line, Ford took a resolute stand against the most elementary improvements. By then Sears Roebuck was offering (in addition to endless gadgets) numerous substitute parts designed to improve its performance, many of which, such as the Sears carburetor, did. Model A was a monument to the tenacity and deviousness by which Ford subordinates managed to get his agreement to a selective slide transmission, hydraulic (or even adequate) brakes, and better tires. These were among the things that made Model A a good car. At the time Ford had no research or engineering organization worthy of the name. His laboratories, all agree, were an empty shell partly because Ford was suspicious of college-trained men. A man of modest mechanical perception, let alone a mechanical genius, would have seen the need for a trained research and engineering organization in the country's largest manufacturing enterprise in one of its most aggressively competitive industries. When, after much trouble and uncertainty, Model A was finally in production, Ford resisted improvements in that.

Nor were these mechanical crotchets confined to the cars. As a young man, Ford worked at the Detroit Edison Illuminating Company in the days when direct current was still in use. He knew that Edison had resisted — unwisely in the event — the introduction of alternating current. By the time the great plant at River Rouge was under construction, DC had long since given way to AC. The latter had formidable advantages in efficiency, economy, and technical adaptability. Ford, nonetheless, insisted that the generators at the Rouge and also the myriad of individual motors which by now had replaced the shafts and pulleys be on DC. His engineers knew he was wrong but dared not oppose him. Eventually the plant had to be changed to AC. The mistake is said to have cost as much as $30,000,000.

Many more examples could be cited. Indeed, it is not going too far to say that between 1920 and his death Ford's resistance to mechanical innovation, and on occasion to mechanical common sense, cost the company hundreds of millions of dollars in sales, the leadership in the automobile industry, and even raised threats to its survival. If this was genius, it was good for General Motors.

7

What, then, is the answer? For it still remains that Henry Ford built the most famous car of all time, certainly the greatest manufacturing enterprise of its day. In an age when so many men are subject to the expansive and expensive attentions of public relations experts, debunking should perhaps be subsidized. But the debunker operates on the phony — the man whose accomplishments are confined to the press releases. Ford's accomplishments are there for all to see. How did a man with such grievous shortcomings do (or become identified with) so much?

One reason is that because the Ford was the first car

most people ever knew, Ford is awarded honors as an inventor he did not entirely deserve. He built and drove his first horseless vehicle in 1896, although not uncharacteristically, in what Nevins calls a blend of "poor memory and wishful thinking," he later made the date "about 1891 and 2." By 1896 dozens of boys and men had done or were doing the same thing. And some had done far more than Ford. The automobile, as Merz and doubtless others have said, was not invented. Engine and chassis were developed over a period of years. Ford was a latecomer. Four years before he wheeled out his car for its dramatic (and subsequently much publicized) midnight run in Detroit, the firm of Panhard and Levassor in Paris had *issued a catalogue* of their line of gasoline-powered cars. Things were less advanced in America — the gasoline buggy which the Duryea brothers drove in 1892 in Springfield, Massachusetts, was far more primitive than the French vehicles — but both they and others were far ahead of Ford.

Ford did build several early cars and made something of a name for himself as a racer. These were considerable achievements, although others did as much who never acquired his reputation. Much of the early difference was almost certainly made by a group of able men — Couzens, Wills and the Dodge Brothers — who joined Ford in the early years of the century to have the benefit of his public name. It is to Ford's credit that he accepted their help. But it would be hard to say whether he selected them or they selected him.

The company made money from the first year. Its cars were no better and no cheaper than those of its competitors, and this was long before the arrival of Model T. In the success of the Ford Motor Company, something must be credited to the indiscriminate enthusiasm with which people bought automobiles. No invention so nearly sold itself. At first Ford did not see any special advantage in a cheap, light car, but later when he did he seized upon it with unequaled tenacity. That Ford was a tenacious man, none can doubt. Then it did him great service. Later it did him equal disservice.

The Model T when it arrived in 1908 was not mechanically ahead of its time nor was it especially inexpensive. But supporting Ford's undoubted conviction that this was the right car were the talents of one of the great organizers of all times — James Couzens. He created the superb dealer organization which sold and serviced the cars. This produced an insistent pressure on the factory and then he organized the production that sought to supply the demand. Ford did not interfere; in these days of almost incredible expansion before the First World War he spent little time at the factory. Sorenson has called these years the "Couzens Period." "Everyone in the company, including Henry Ford, acknowledged his as the driving force during this period." [11] In contrast with Ford, Couzens never gave a sign of being impressed by his achievement.

After Couzens left in 1915, Ford took full command, and the company was never so successful again. It was partly the prestige and fame which success had brought to his name which caused Ford to assume control, and Couzens resigned partly because he felt that Ford wished to use the

[11] *My Forty Years With Ford,* p. 36.

business as his personal advertisement. In the years that followed, Ford was a relentless and avid self-advertiser. And he mobilized the efforts of many others to promote not the car but the man. Only the multitude remained unaware of the effort which Ford, both deliberately and instinctively, devoted to building the Ford myth. He seemed such an unassuming man. He was the first and by far the most successful product of public relations in industry.

Finally, a word can be said in explanation of at least some of his mistakes. Ford was born in 1863. He emerged as a national figure in 1914, the year of the five-dollar day, when he was fifty-one. Many of the mistakes which contradict his claim to stature were made after that. Any reasonable view of Ford must reckon with the fact that, in the years when the light beat hardest upon him, he was past his prime. Success had made him immune to counsel and advice; for too long he had seen eccentricity and even mere foolishness pictured as genius and had believed it.

Part Three

The Nostalgic Farmer

X

The Pleasures and Uses of Bankruptcy

SINCE THE END of World War II, we have been coming for the summer to an old farm in southeastern Vermont. Once here, the days lengthen perceptibly. There is magic in the late evening mist on our meadows and the way the early morning sun comes through the maples. Life acquires a new tranquillity. So, we think, do the children. The pay, entertainment allowances and other perquisites of a professor compare badly with those of industry, law and harness racing. But it is hard to regret an occupation which enables one to spend three or four months of each year on the edge of paradise. Many others yearn for such privileged surroundings and therein lies the story.

As a teacher of economics, I am visited each summer by a certain number of my professional friends and colleagues. Without exception, they inquire about the economic underpinning of this part of Vermont. Some are being polite; some may even wish to know. I have found the line of thought which these questions set in motion to be troublesome. The hills and narrow valleys north of the Massachusetts line and between the Green Mountains and the Connecticut look reasonably prosperous but they are without visible means of support. There are no important industries — fortunately. The valleys have a few dairy farms, but it is northern Vermont which fattens on the revenues and suffers the vicissitudes of the Boston milkshed. Some people work in the forests which have largely retrieved the stony and never very fertile cropland. But this is too rigorous an occupation for many of my neighbors. French Canadians are considered better suited to such toil. For a year or two, as this is written, a considerable number have been employed in building two large federal flood-control dams in the neighborhood, but people were fairly prosperous before the Army Engineers made things better. Many local residents have always worked on the roads — scraping them and repairing winter damage in the summer and plowing the snow in the winter. But my best-informed neighbor says that all of the money so earned goes back in taxes for keeping up the roads. I haven't checked his calculations, but he is a reliable man.

Then there are the part-time residents — on the whole, we would rather be called "part-time residents" than "summer people" because, as compared with Maine or Martha's Vineyard, we arrive earlier in the summer and stay much later in the autumn, so we are really part of the community. But this is not a fashionable area, and the migratory population consists either of professors or businessmen who share the interests of their academic friends, including an interest in not wasting money. We contribute something to the economic life, but we are no gold mine.

✿

2

But gradually I have become aware of another source of revenue which is important. And those who supply it add greatly to the comfort, convenience and pleasure of country life and may even make it tolerable. These are the people who systematically disburse their savings, money they have inherited or whatever they can borrow, on enterprises conducted for the public good. They grow things, make useful articles or (most important of all) render valuable services which one could never obtain on a purely commercial basis. Their prices are not always low, but since they are always selling below cost, no one can complain. The community benefits not only from the goods and services they supply but also from the rent or interest they pay, the purchases they make, and the payrolls they meet. To be sure, the day comes when the rent, interest, bills and payroll become troublesome or can no longer be met. But, invariably others come along. The competition to serve the public at a loss is rather keen. In a town not far from here is an inn which has failed decisively in the financial sense not once but twice in the past five years. It is now up for sale at the highest price yet. The chances of getting the asking price or something close are excellent. On the basis of this and other cases, it is my belief that service generally improves with each bankruptcy.

Inns provide the best example of capital consumption, to give this admirable phenomenon its technical name. In the course of an autumn holiday, to offer what economists call a synthetic model of reality, a man and his wife from

New Canaan take a leisurely motor trip to Montreal. They are fond of the country, which is why they live in Fairfield County and why they choose this particular trip. Somewhere between Brattleboro and Montpelier they spend a night at a village inn on a secondary road — not a motel, but the real thing with elms and maples all but hiding the small Shell station across the way. What peace! What a contrast between the life of the innkeepers and their own! Independence and serenity as against the daily penance on the New Haven, the obscene struggle on the subway and the crushing pressures of organization.

The travelers have talked of getting off the rat-race. Could it really happen? It won't happen to many people, but it could happen to them. This husband has about fifteen years before actuarial decrepitude, the sense to know it, and a keen desire to enjoy the years that remain. His wife is younger and a good companion. They have some money. They have something even more precious, which is imagination and courage and a knowledge of how to cook.

Vaguely, perhaps more than vaguely, they know that the trend is away from the great corporations. The small entrepreneur has always been morally superior — a true child of freedom. Liberal Democrats support him to the hilt. He is not the sort of man Ike had to the White House in the heyday of modern Republicanism. But he is esteemed by *Fortune* which regularly publishes vignettes of small business ingenuity, enterprise and success. Quite a number of these tell of men who found fulfillment and success by starting on their own very late in life. None tells of failure. Those of us who profit from the savings of people who are going broke are profoundly indebted to these and similar success stories and the overtones of community stature, moral fiber, social responsibility and easy money which they contain. The couple returns to the village and searches out the real estate man. He is not hard to find.

"Yes, there is a good small inn for sale." It turns out to be the one at which they stopped. This is no coincidence; nearly all small country inns are for sale. Being from New York and therefore experienced in the tools of modern management, the husband has a good hard look at the books. He finds that it has been losing money. Perceptively and quite correctly, he attributes the losses to bad management. What he does not know is that such enterprises never make enough money to give the impression even of indifferent management.

So the previous owners go back to New Jersey. For four years, they have furnished jobs and modest wages to the community. They have bought meat and frozen vegetables from the local grocer and quite a bit of liquor from the state store. There were moments when it seemed possible that the liquor might put them in the black and other less commercial interludes when it eased toil and softened anxiety. The part-time residents have had a place with atmosphere and home cooking at which to dine and, on occasion, to deposit a redundant guest. During the two-week deer season and the week before Labor Day, business was always amazing — several times what could be accommodated. The total cost of so benefiting the community was $13,600. It would have been more but, because of the competition to serve, they are selling out at a considerable capital gain.

They have also provided us with considerable unpaid labor, although it is the capital that really counts.

The future is also bright. The local carpenter and his two men can look forward to the busiest autumn since the other couple from New Jersey converted their barn into a full-time furniture factory. For the new owners of the inn have unhesitantly identified better management with modernizing the kitchen, refurnishing the bedrooms, adding two baths, and making the former woodshed into a cozy new bar. These improvements will make the inn a better place to leave or take guests and more of an all-round community asset.

3

Lest anyone think this story contrived, let me return to strict matters of experience. For years, we have been eating meals at a succession of inns that were being endowed by their owners. The owners were from the city. All were able to bring a modest amount of capital to our service. We always guessed that they were spending money on us and this could have meant — there are some subtle differences here between average and marginal costs — that each visit absorbed some of their capital. Nonetheless, we always felt that our patronage was a real favor and so did they. We were always sorry to see them go, as eventually they did, but we were comforted by the knowledge that others would take their place, and others always have.

Until last year, our plumbing was done by a man from Long Island, who left suddenly for (I believe) Montana. We have some excellent and very inexpensive furniture from a former furniture factory. I owe a dollar and fifty cents for some white gladioli to a man who also disappeared and before I could pay him. A nice neighbor left his job in New York to drill artesian wells. We would have patronized him, but unhappily he went out of business just before we ran out of water. Some time ago, I negotiated for a piece of property with a former Army colonel who had left his job on Wall Street to enter the local real estate business. When I suggested that the price was too high, he said I had mortally insulted his professional honor as a West Pointer, and the deal fell through. He is now back in a bond house. We used to sell our hay to a horse farm which provided an excellent market while it lasted. We get firewood from people — they change frequently — who believe that their forest is a real resource. A neighbor from New York is supplying us with potatoes. He is an encouraging departure, for he is not using savings or an inheritance but has one foot in an advertising agency. The list of such benefactors could be extended almost indefinitely.

4

The notion of an economic system in which everyone works hard, saves his money, and then disperses it by running useful enterprises for the common good is very attractive. However, the local Vermonters do not participate to any extent. They have a strong preference for profitable activity. This means they are rarely to be found running country inns, making furniture, growing African violets (an especially imaginative current venture) or raising horses or potatoes. U.S. Route 5 makes its way along the eastern border of the state through a hideous neon-lighted tunnel walled by motels, antique shops, roadside furniture shops featuring not Vermont but North Carolina craftsmanship and, of course, service stations and restaurants. Quite a few local people are to be found here for they have discovered that the Humbert Humberts patronize this garish bazaar in preference to the lovely local villages, as does almost everyone else. There are no New Yorkers on Route 5. One can hardly trade the rat race for a multiple-lane highway.

As a nation, we owe much to subsidies. They built the railroads, and also the airlines. Advocates of protection have never wavered in their belief that it was tariff subsidies — as distinct from, say, free competition — which made our country industrially great. Our merchant marine is kept afloat by a subsidy, and so, we may recall, was Richard Nixon in his salad days. Evidently, therefore, we need feel no shame that our pleasant countryside is subsidized by aspiring small enterprisers. And as subsidies go, this is an excellent one. Unlike farm support prices, it requires no federal appropriations and brings no charges that we are living too well at the taxpayers' expense. Unlike the depletion allowances enjoyed by the oilmen, it brings no complaints, quite justified, of fantastic favoritism. Our subsidy is perfectly reliable, for as I have noted, when one entrepreneur has exhausted his capital and credit, another is always ready and eager to take his place. The very best journals proclaim the virtue of such sacrifice on our behalf. It is a demonstration of worth, an affirmation of faith in the system. A recession or depression would, one imagines, increase the number of people seeking the serenity of the country and the security of their own business. The outlays must have a certain cogency to the individuals involved, but this has nothing to do with the great impersonal sweep of economic forces.

XI

Farming an Abandoned Farm

FOR SOME YEARS I have been conducting an informal and highly unprofessional investigation of the New England farm real estate market. My interest, like that of nearly all of the customers for such property, has been in the farms that cannot or should not be farmed. It has occurred to me that I should make these findings more generally available, but I do so without any intention of trying to save the prospective purchaser money. I would like to see him invest in New England real estate — I regard this as good for New England, for the value of some land that I own myself, and also good for the purchaser. However, while I have a few suggestions about how to keep the investment within reasonable bounds, anyone for whom saving money is a paramount consideration should keep it in the bank.

2

Each autumn in this part of southern Vermont people who visited friends in the country in the summer decide that they must have a place of their own by next year. They owe it to the children and there is no nicer time to look than on autumn weekends when the maples are turning. To this seasonal demand for country real estate is added that of two other groups, more or less permanently in the market.

The first and most numerous of the nonseasonal home-seekers consist of people who are in retreat from the city, mostly from New York. Local real estate men realize that their fortunes are tied up with New York City's traffic congestion and the state of its transit system. In the line of duty they read the New York papers and view the future with confidence.

Along with the fugitives from the subway come the advance refugees from the bombs — those who have convinced themselves that it might be possible to sustain life for a month or two in the New England hills after New York, Boston, and maybe also Brattleboro, Vermont and Keene, New Hampshire, have been vaporized. This demand fluctuates with the warmth of the cold war and of late — in spite of the stern warnings from Washington that we must not relax — it has been falling off. However, with the world as it is, this recession may be only temporary.

3

Unlike the futures market, which most people merely do not understand, the trouble with the New England Abandoned Farms Market is that most of what is understood is wrong.

First there is the notion that the hills and valleys of New England have now been combed over and all the nice old houses with a view have been snatched up. It is true that you can no longer find a lovely old colonial, shabby but sound, with four fireplaces, nice meadows, stately maples, a brook, and a distant mountain for fifteen hundred dollars. However, there is still an abundance of less graceful houses with a view that, if unspectacular, is better than anything in the East Sixties. With the land thrown in, they offer, for these days, exceptionally inexpensive if somewhat imperfect shelter. In Vermont and New Hampshire the person with from nothing to, say, seven thousand dollars doesn't have much choice. If he has from eight to twelve thousand dollars he can spend many happy days traveling around the back roads with the local real estate men, confident in the knowledge that he is a very decent prospect.

The market is also still being replenished. New England is no longer a declining agricultural region. The long period of decay which started in 1825 when the Erie Canal began admitting cheap Ohio grain to the East has been arrested for twenty-five years or more. But while dairying, broiler raising, and fruit, vegetable, and tobacco production have been expanding in favored locations, farm abandonment in the hill towns has continued. Most of the houses, to be frank, are pretty tacky by the time the last occupant dies or moves to town. But so, originally, was that darling place the Greens bought and fixed up.

4

A second misconception is that buying real estate is an outrageously risky business. For the first two or three centuries of our history it was taken for granted that city people were smarter than country folk. Countless yokels were victimized each year by accomplished urban students of devious if somewhat stylized fraud. Now, with O. Henry, the chronicler of this larceny, only fifty years in his grave, the tables have been completely turned. The city man, and especially the New Yorker, is regarded as a commercial cretin. And he so regards himself. He does not think for a moment that he is a match for the amiable villager whose rough-hewn and battered exterior masks a capacity for the deepest guile. To buy real estate from such a man is, he feels, to risk total expropriation.

There is always a chance that in buying an old farm one will fall into the hands of some rural Raffles, but the danger is not great. For one thing, the risks in buying an old farm dwelling are minor. Warnings about morbid beams, rotten sills, and leaky roofs have been greatly overdone. If anything is seriously wrong it will be evident to the eye even of the most innocent purchaser. If something goes wrong it can either be left that way or if — like a leak in the roof — it is too uncomfortable it can be patched.

And much can be wrong without being fatal. I had a Harvard colleague who spent each summer enjoying a breathtaking view of the Green Mountains from a house that had had no maintenance of any kind for at least fifty years. Something fell off each year. And the house looked as though it might fall in — visiting assistant professors were reported as feeling encouraged about their chances for early promotion. But it didn't fall in and won't.

It is true that rural real estate men ask marvelously inflated prices from their suburban colleagues on the bare chance that an utter idiot will come along and pay the first sum mentioned. But a little inquiry in the neighborhood will always establish a consensus on what the old place is worth. The neighbors will help, partly because they don't want to see anyone get robbed and partly because they have a deep mistrust of the real estate man who makes a living without decent labor.

5

The grave threat to your pocketbook comes not from the seller or his much maligned agent but from yourself, and the dangerous time is after you have bought. Once you are in possession you will yield to the impulse to improve. This means a water system, a better kitchen, the removal of a partition or two, sanding to bring out the "natural beauty" of the old floors, a terrace, a rambler rose, a workshop and a dam.

The impulse to improve cannot be resisted; it is American and doubtless made us what we are today. The only hope is to divert it into inexpensive channels. The best thing is paint. Paint is not expensive; the results of an hour's work are admirably visible to the naked eye. Structural flaws, when well-groomed, may acquire an antiquarian interest.

An inexpensive alternative to painting is cutting brush. Among the marvels of New England is its phenomenal pro-creation of young trees — "God loves this country," an old neighbor of mine remarks, "and He is always trying to get it back." Once you are persuaded that brush anywhere in the near or middle distance is an eyesore and have equipped yourself with a brushhook you are also tolerably well pro-tected from spending money.

Thus, the urge to improve need not be resisted, for it can be sublimated. The urge to farm, though less universal, is fiscally much more dangerous. It must be checked and checked with the utmost firmness.

The reasons for not trying to revive an abandoned farm would seem to be fairly apparent. After all, it was abandoned. The last farmer may not have been the kind of operator on whom the county agent dotes, but if the farm had been good he might have been a better farmer. Or a better farmer might have rescued the farm. Instead it went out of business. So have thousands of New England farms. Yet typically it is only a short step from the acquisition of an old farm to a state of deep sorrow that such beautiful terrain should lie commercially derelict. The new owner resolves, with far more heroism than he suspects, to hold a bridgehead against those inscrutable economic forces which have been returning New England to timber.

If the decision is to tackle dairying or chickens, one cannot absolutely predict failure. In the right locations and in the hands of competent managers dairying and poultry raising do succeed. However the entrepreneur's success would be considerably more probable if he were not a new arrival and had selected the farm initially with these enterprises in mind.

But dairying and modern poultry husbandry are demanding and — because of somewhat undignified chores — unromantic agriculture. Accordingly, the man who has caught the fatal vision of redeeming New England from the birch and maple and pine and wild cherry is much more likely to think of a herd of Aberdeen Angus cattle or a flock of Shropshire sheep moving placidly over his meadows. Or if he prides himself on his imagination, his mind may leap on to some really novel enterprise — an apiary or a nursery or geese.

Here one can be dogmatic. If a particular type of agriculture is not being practiced in New England it is roughly a hundred to one that it is because it doesn't pay. And it is at least a thousand to one that any successful new enterprise will be hit upon by some intelligent and skillful local farmer in consultation with the Extension Service and not by a new arrival from town.

6

Take the case of sheep. Except on a few mixed farms in northern New England, the sheep population of this area is negligible. Every year several hundred new arrivals from town are stunned by this oversight. They see plenty of rough pasture everywhere. Sheep, they know, are notoriously untroubled by steep hillsides, stones and streams. The yield of forage on such pasture is anywhere from five to fifty times that which supports the flocks that once supported Senator McCarran. Sheep leave the meadows clipped and groomed and free of brush — "Remember how beautiful the hills in the Lake Country around Windermere are?"

As an agricultural economist, in the face of the advantages just listed, I have never succeeded in making a case against sheep raising to any determined sheep raiser. Still there are a few disadvantages to be mentioned.

New England pastures, while lush in the summer, are singularly unavailable in the winter. That means New England must compete with areas that have year-round pasture or, at least, do not have to go in for prolonged winter feeding. Since New England produces almost no grain, concentrates for finishing lambs must be imported from the Midwest, whereas Iowa farms can fatten lambs on grain grown in the adjacent field.

Fencing is also necessary — a stone wall is no barrier to a determined ewe — and this is expensive. Fences will not keep out dogs, of which New England has an unusually dense population, and their owners dislike having them shot. In the Mountain and Midwestern States men who can shear sheep or lend an experienced hand at lambing time can be found, but these arts are all but unknown in the Berkshires and the Green Mountains.

Finally, sheep husbandry is a declining industry in the nation at large. While Nevada has a decided edge on New Hampshire, it competes poorly with Australia. In Canada, when I was a youngster, a good flock of sheep would pay the taxes. The most that can be expected of them in New England is a sizable income tax deduction.

If resistance to ostensible land utilization is out of the question, the owner of abandoned farm land has one possibility that will cost little. That is to grow trees. The investment in forest management is small; the return is reasonably secure. There is a county forester who will advise. It also makes sense, something which does not impress visitors but often increases a man's stature in the eyes of his neighbors.

❁

7

With self-control and an enlightened preference for forestry over agriculture, the cost of owning an old farm in New England need not greatly exceed that of owning and garaging an automobile in New York City. (Taxes are still low — those on a hundred acres and an old house will rarely be as much as the insurance on the car.)

It is the peculiar good fortune of the New Yorker, and indeed of everyone who lives along the eastern seaboard, that he is close to an erstwhile agricultural region. Poor land makes good scenery. An ancient farmhouse, as a weekend or holiday retreat, is in wonderfully mellow contrast with the raw log and shingle affairs which people must build for themselves among the Minnesota lakes or in the national forests. It is most unlikely that anyone who ever bought one didn't become sublimely proud both of himself and his property.

XII

The Wholesome Influence

ONE PLEASANT summer day in 1959 when, fortunately, little else was happening, the newspapers broke into a mild rash of joy over the announcement of the prospective birth of another member of the British royal family. The *New York Times* had a special story headed, LONDON IS AGOG, which said, "There was great excitement everywhere, in shops, pubs, and buildings. Friends hailed one another with the simple greeting: 'Isn't it wonderful news?' or 'I told you so.' "

One didn't know of course how many people exchanged these simple greetings; it is possible that the correspondent had a fairly well-developed sense for what people in shops, pubs, and also buildings are supposed to say on such occasions. However, I found myself comparing this enthusiasm, actual or improved, with the response which similar news would have produced (or failed to produce) in the circles in which I moved as a youngster. Nostalgia carries one back on wings.

The scene of the contrasting reaction to royalty was in the county of Elgin on the north shore of Lake Erie in what was still quite unabashedly called the British Empire, and the ethnic situation is important. Large parts of what is now

the Province of Ontario were settled from the Scotch High-
lands in the first half of the last century and quite a bit of
Elgin County was so populated about a hundred and thirty
years ago. In my youth there were many roads where the
only families without the prefix "Mac" to their surnames
were the Camerons, the Grahams, and the Robbs. On some
there was a clear majority of MacCallums, nearly all of them
named John, and distinguished only by nicknames that were
often offensive. In the northern part of the township where
I was born, there was a solid settlement of Campbells
grouped, not inappropriately, around a town called Camp-
bellton.

2

Had my neighbors been accused of disloyalty to the Crown,
they would have denied it. They did not strike such attitudes, especially on matters of no pressing importance. But
one could be loyal and still have grave misgivings about the
royal establishment. That was the case.

History was the source of some of the doubts. A number
of the Scots who came to Canada in the century following
the Battle of Culloden did so to escape what they believed to
be English persecution of the clans. And it is likely that
some who came out of purely fiscal motives developed a
loftier explanation after the fact. By my time most of this
had been forgotten in the heavy work of clearing away the
hardwood forests and making the land into farms. But there
remained the vague feeling that the English and their rulers
had been unkind to our ancestors. It is true that if the matter
were pressed too far, some retarded historian might have
mentioned the beheading of Mary Queen of Scots.

More important in shaping these attitudes was the famous (to Canadians) Family Compact of the early part of the nineteenth century. This was a small closely knit oligarchy which, during the years of settlement, dominated the political, ecclesiastical and commercial life of Upper Canada for its own unquestioned profit. At its apex were the governing officials of the Crown, posts which were considered especially suitable for retired British generals regardless of qualification. Inside, automatically, was anyone of aristocratic lineage or some reasonable substitute. One popular substitute was a passionate and articulate devotion to the Queen and all the royal family. Mostly outside were the Scotch. The insiders believed with reason that the monarchy was a buttress of their political, social and financial privileges and never ceased to admire and defend it for that reason. This made it hard for the Scotch to be equally royal, and they were not.

With the passage of time, and especially after the Confederation of the provinces into the fully self-governing Dominion in 1867, the Scotch gained political equality and something approaching social acceptability. But the old attitudes and animosities persisted. Until well along in this century, the city of Toronto yielded to none in the entire Empire or Commonwealth in its adoration of royalty out to and including the most distant royal duke. Still visible on the Toronto skyline is a castle built by a rich and worried magnate who was oppressed by the thought that there was no place Edward VII could stay in suitable state were he to visit Canada. The rich and well-born continuing to feel this way, it was natural that others should continue to feel otherwise. Rural Elgin contained no rich and certainly no well-born. Many of its political attitudes, including the marked preference of the farmers for the Liberal Party, traced to the time of the Family Compact.

3

Of greater immediate importance were the questions of expense and drink.

The first was quite straightforward. Apart from an infinitesimal amount to support the Governors General, who if not royal were always impressively regal, Canadians paid no taxes to support the monarchy. But my neighbors disliked unnecessary expense even when it was shouldered by Englishmen. My earliest political recollection is of debate over the cost of the royal establishment — the numerous palaces, carriages, servants and the royal yacht. Neil MacAlpine, an authority on many matters, thought the total might run to two or three thousand dollars a day or, say, a hundred dollars for every hour of the twenty-four. This was staggering, and Neil may have been the real originator of the calculations which now tell us what the Federal Government costs each time the clock ticks. In what was assumed to be sound public relations for the Crown, newspapers like the *Toronto Mail and Empire* carried accounts of the royal progresses from Buckingham to Windsor to Sandringham to Balmoral. In our circles, this only added to the impression of intolerable expense.

The question of drink was more complicated. The royal family was believed to be bibulous. I do not know the grounds for this. Perhaps it owed something to the expansive personality of Edward VII. I do recall my father, who tried to be fair-minded about such matters, saying there was no evidence that George V drank as much as Edward did. The impression may also have owed something to the appearance of some of the Governors General, the representatives of the King in Canada. To the not untutored eyes of the local experts, they looked like men who were given to belting a bottle. Some were.

In this community everyone was ardently opposed to liquor, an aversion which was firmly grounded on the manner of its consumption. In the neighboring town of Dutton, there were two hotels — the Queens Hotel and the more felicitously named McIntyre House. Every Saturday night until World War I, a small but rugged segment of the community gathered under the tolerant sign of the Clan McIntyre for that most arduous of entertainments, a bloody Scottish saturnalia. At least that is how they were described by those who did not attend. And from time to time fights did break out with broken whiskey bottles as the weapons and these, it was known locally, could do damage to the complexion even of a MacPherson.

Drinking, therefore, was identified with these mortal assaults on the peace. Since everyone, including the participants when sober, greatly deplored them, anyone who was addicted to strong drink was suspect, and there was no local experience with any other kind. No one imagined that George V, were he to show up at the McIntyre House of a Saturday evening, would be found brandishing a bottle and challenging the Campbells to combat. But, by one of the more remote forms of guilt by association, he was identified with such behavior.

Proximity to the United States also had some effect on our attitudes. Countries, like people, gain in distinction and self-esteem by reflecting on the things which make them different from their associates. Canadians have always reflected with considerable pride on the things — the impeccable judiciary, the parliamentary system, the two languages, the rich minerals, the rugged climate — which differentiate them from their nearest associate, the United States. And many have thought the possession of a King or Queen a considerable point. In Elgin, however, we were only about a hundred miles from Detroit. And among our average-born, this city, so far from being regarded with anything like jealousy, was an object of undisguised admiration. When autumn came and the work on the farms slackened, the more enterprising youths made for Windsor. There they entrusted their suit-cases to some friends who crossed the border regularly and thus had nothing to fear from the immigration men. Then they crossed informally, explaining, if asked, that they were on their way to one of the movies or burlesque houses up Woodward Avenue from the ferry. After a winter on the assembly line, they returned with a more interesting ward-robe, a pocketful of money and an assured position for the summer on a social pyramid which, however, had as its apex not King George but Henry Ford.

4

All of these tendencies were well known, though their existence was never openly conceded, by those who stood four-square for the monarchy. And corrective measures were taken. At this time the ardor of the Toronto Tories was still reflected in the schoolbooks, and at the normal schools it was made clear to the fledgling teachers that they should inculcate a love for King and country with considerable emphasis on the former. We sang "God Save the King" in school (along with "The Maple Leaf Forever") and sometimes we were allowed to sing the now suppressed stanza which respectfully requested God to undertake sabotage and political subversion inside the ranks of the King's enemies. Once or twice each year we were visited by the school inspector appointed for Elgin County by the Province of Ontario. A staunch imperialist named Mr. Taylor, he felt it his duty to offset the dubious home environment of the pupils (and some teachers) by always concluding his visit with a speech extolling the wisdom and virtue of the royal family and their warm feeling for every last one of us.

George V, as it was perhaps recognized, was not a figure with an instant appeal to school children. And Queen Mary was impressive at the price of being alarming, at least to anyone from a Canadian farm. Her pictures always showed six or eight strands of pearls wrapped tightly around her neck. One of the girls in school, a thoughtful lass named Edna MacColl, had the interesting theory that these controlled a severe case of goiter and had to be worn night as well as day.

However, if the King and Queen lacked something in warmth and friendly appeal, the situation was completely redeemed, in the years following World War I, by the Prince of Wales, later Edward VIII and still later and more durably, the Duke of Windsor. The Prince was then fresh from the terrible fighting on the Western Front which, unlike so many Canadians, he had by some miracle survived. (We knew at the time that it was high military policy to use Canadian troops to spearhead attacks. We did not know that the policy on the Prince was pretty much the reverse.) In addition to being brave, the Prince was good, cheerful, deeply concerned about the welfare of his father's subjects, a keen student of the history and geography of the Empire, devoted to his parents and brothers and sister, and full of much innocent fun. The question of alcohol did not arise. The word most often used to describe the Prince was "wholesome," which automatically excluded drinking and any other serious sin. Even criticism on grounds of expense was partly forestalled. The Prince soon purchased a cattle ranch in Alberta which seemed to show a willingness to earn at least part of his keep.

5

Whether by accident or design, the postwar summer and autumn of 1919 brought to a kind of crescendo the effort to make the royal family both a living and constructive influence in our lives. In mid-August, the Prince arrived at St. John, New Brunswick, for an extended tour of the Dominion and was greeted by populace, dignitaries, and nine beautiful young girls, all dressed in white presumably to symbolize wholesomeness, each bearing the shield of one of the Canadian provinces. There and in many more addresses in the weeks following, the Prince was warmly praised for his heroic role in the hostilities just ended. His replies adverting accurately to "the modest part which I was able to play in the great war" were taken to signify an almost unbelievably unassuming nature. He did, however, frequently recur to the theme that his knowledge of "the splendid nations of the British Empire was formed, gentlemen, in the trenches, camps, and billets of the Western Front."

The Prince went roughing it in the Lake Nipigon country, piloted a train, spontaneously greeted a Labor Day parade in Ottawa, saw farms and factories, and, if he ever deviated for a moment from the behavior befitting an Eagle Scout, we certainly did not hear of it. And checking my memory on these matters a few weeks ago, I discovered that even older hands were impressed. The *New York Times* correspondent who covered the tour wired from Winnipeg an extended account of the Prince's visit to the Grain Exchange where he inquired into the mysteries of trade and bought and sold some ordinary or tame oats. As the royal visitor made his way across the pit, the *Times* man, in those days also a chap with a keen ear as well as a gift for language, heard such comments as "A fine kiddo"; "A regular feller"; "He'll do"; and "A manly looking chap." "He shows," the reporter said, "an active curiosity for all such workaday facts and feels the modern sense of the romanticity of such matters." This would seem to mean that he had an exceptionally wholesome curiosity.

It is not surprising that during all of that year we had a large picture of the Prince of Wales in British officer's dress on the front wall of school. Tacked up next to it was an essay by Edna MacColl which had been read and warmly commended on the occasion of a visit by Mr. Taylor and which was entitled "Why We Love Our Good Prince Charming." I have forgotten the contents except that it combined a prayer for his good health with the practical suggestion that he give up riding horses. At the time, the Prince was having some difficulty staying up.

This was at school. At home, things were very different. In our case, neither the Prince nor his parents were welcome as topics of conversation. Perhaps they were part of the price of free public education. If so, the payment was sufficiently rendered in school.

6

It was in the process of learning why even such a paragon as the Prince could not usefully be mentioned at home that I learned my father's position. A former schoolteacher, and a considerable figure in the political life of West Elgin, he passed over the trivia of expense along with the alcohol. He did not entirely deny George V a certain role as a link with history. It gave some added meaning to Elizabeth, Charles I, and Victoria to have a successor still in office. But it was very poor business to have at the head of the state a man whose vast prestige was the purest accident of parentage. Legitimatize such accidents there and you excused them everywhere. It helped sanction even the pretensions and possibly the prices of the local drygoods hierarchy in Dutton itself. If the Prince were all that he was cracked up to be, he would have no difficulty qualifying for the succession in open competitive examination. If he lost out, it would be to a better man. I have never been able to see the defects in this argument.

In the summer of 1959, just before the awesome announcement which stimulated this flow of recollection, the Queen and Prince Philip made a royal progress through Canada. There had been many since the visit of the Prince. There were complaints of indifference toward this one on the part of my former compatriots. (There were also complaints about Canadians who said there was indifference.) Some of my Canadian friends thought it might be the last such visit. The tour wasn't a failure; by the arcane standards by which such rituals are appraised, it might even have been a mild success. But lurking just below the surface, some think, was the possibility of trouble, which is to say a display of obvious disinterest. On the other hand, Chicago, the source of Mayor Thompson's famous assault on our same George V, gave the royal couple a notable welcome.

This seemed to me understandable and reassuring. My Canadian contemporaries and their children were still pondering how it would all work out in a competitive examination. Chicago, which had never been so privileged before, was responding in a most encouraging fashion to a wholesome influence.

N. A. S. BRUNSWICK. ME.